THE

HIJACKING

of JESUS

THE

HIJACKING

of JESUS

How the Religious Right Distorts Christianity
and Promotes Violence and Hate

Dan Wakefield

NATION
BOOKS

THE HIJACKING OF JESUS
How the Religious Right Distorts Christianity and Promotes Violence and Hate

Published by
Nation Books
An Imprint of Avalon Publishing Group Inc.
245 West 17th Street, 11th Floor
New York, NY 10011

AVALON
publishing group incorporated

First printing March 2006

Library of Congress Cataloging-in-Publication Data is available.

ISBN: 1-56025-745-8
ISBN 13: 978-1-56025-745-5

9 8 7 6 5 4 3 2 1

Book design by Maria E. Torres
Printed in the United States of America
Distributed by Publishers Group West

To Maureen Langer

CONTENTS

I.

The Armies of the Right

The religious war going on in this country today is not just about religion anymore, nor is it limited to politics or even "culture." It is about the future of the United States of America, and I don't mean some hazy, far-off dream, but the immediate as well as the long-term life of you and your family, your colleagues and friends, your work and your private life.

Christianity in this country has become almost synonymous with right-wing fanaticism, conservative politics and—courtesy of Mel Gibson—a brutally sadistic version of religious experience. Millions of Christians like me are appalled by this distortion of our faith, which only three decades ago stood for peace, equality, healing, and compassion for society's outcasts—the issues that comprised the ministry of Jesus.

When I say "I'm a Christian," I feel the need to explain myself: I'm not one of "them," the ones who fit the image of the faith that you see in the headlines now. I read stories and headlines almost every day using the term "Christians" that presume to reflect the views of those of us who belong to mainline Protestant denominations, or who are progressive Evangelicals or politically liberal Catholics, but reflect only the actions and opinions of denominations and sects that march to the beat of the Religious Right.

The description "The Hijacking of Jesus" was coined by the activist writer-editor Jim Wallis, founder and editor of *Sojourners*, a "progressive" Evangelical magazine ("progressive" has become the more acceptable term in our political lexicon now that the right has succeeded in making "liberal" a label of political darkness, a brand of the Devil). "An enormous misrepresentation of Christianity has taken place," Wallis wrote in his recent bestseller *God's Politics: Why the Right Gets It Wrong and the Left Doesn't Get It,* "many people around the world now think that Christian faith stands for political commitments that are almost the opposite of its true meaning. How did the faith of Jesus come to be known as prorich, prowar, and pro-American?"

The Jesus of the Gospels had no possessions, ministered to the poor and the sick, befriended society's outcasts, blessed "the peacemakers," and told a wealthy young fellow that a rich man had as much chance of getting into heaven as a camel did of passing through the eye of a needle.

This book is about how the faith of my fathers (my father's father was a Baptist minister in Shelbyville, Kentucky, and Columbia, South Carolina) has been turned upside down to become a cultish kind of Christianity as dangerous as it is distorted, co-opted in the service of a right-wing political agenda that it serves and is served by for the greater profit and power of the billionaires who founded and finance its supportive foundations and institutions. We are in the midst of what Bill Moyers, in the *New York Review of Books*, had called:

> a political holy war financed by wealthy economic interests and guided by savvy partisan operatives who know that couching political ambition in religious rhetoric can ignite the passion of followers as ferociously as when Constantine painted the sign of Christ on the shields of his soldiers and on the banners of his legions and routed his rivals in Rome.

This is a social and economic as well as a religious and political revolution whose tactics include the economic undermining of the American middle class and the further disenfranchisement of the poor while making the superwealthy even wealthier and, beyond that, increasing U.S. power in the rest of the world, now primarily in the Middle East. If the latter ambition leads to Armageddon, well, that too is seen as a goal of a religiously distorted wing of this movement, which believes such world annihilation will bring a thousand-year reign of Christ on earth. This is the preaching being popularized by the Left Behind books that are the top bestsellers in America, hitting sixty million at last count, making Stephen King seem (in horror imagination as well as sales) a piker.

This is also a book about the efforts to challenge the bullying domination of the Religious Right and to reclaim the Jesus of the Sermon on the Mount and the Christianity that led and inspired social and political movements of equality, peace, and justice in this country. Just as the origins of the right-wing religious and political takeover can be traced to the Republican defeat of 1964, so the first serious signs of resurgence of liberal religious forces were born in the shock of the 2004 triumph of George W. Bush and the realization that Rove, Cheney, and the billionaires behind them were settling in for the long-term completion of their revolution.

This religious-political revolution is personal—as personal as your own body, your own bedroom, your own office, your children's schoolroom or college classroom. Sometimes the divisive messages that split our society come in Sunday sermons; sometimes they come in the mail.

In the midst of writing these words, I received a letter from John Ashcroft. Curious to learn what message our former U.S. attorney general under George W. Bush was sending me—a liberal Democrat and member of the United Church of Christ (a progressive Protestant denomination that voted at its 2005 convention to perform gay marriages)—I quickly tore open the envelope, hoping there was not a summons inside.

"Dear Friend," the letter begins, and identifies its author as "a former professor" concerned about our schools and universities failing to educate our youth about American history. Mr. Ashcroft cites, among other distressing statistics, that while 98 percent of our eighteen-to-twenty-four-year-olds "can identify 'Gangsta' rap artist Snoop Doggy Dogg," only 32 percent of that age group "can correctly identify the core words of the Gettysburg address and its timeless message."

(Frankly, the 32 percent of young people who "can correctly identify the core words of the Gettysburg address" seems encouragingly high in a country where 12 percent of the population think Joan of Arc was married to Noah, the man who built the Ark.)

To remedy this situation, Mr. Ashcroft invites me to "Strike back against the liberals that hold contempt for you and your values by becoming a Founder of the Center for the Study of American Civic Literacy with your tax deductible gift to ISI [Intercollegiate Studies Institute, a right-wing foundation]" of $500, $250, $100, $50, "or even $25," as well as signing a statement of support.

On a separate page for pledging a donation (on this page, boxes are provided to check for those who wish to contribute up to $10,000) and signing the statement of support, there is a "Call to Action." This explains that "much more important for the cause of liberty" even than your tax deductible donation is "that you take the following actions. (And we strongly urge you to do so.)"

The first action Mr. Ashcroft recommends is to call your alma mater or any schools or universities in your area to urge them to promote the principals of America's founding: "limited government, free enterprise, individual liberty, and Judeo-Christian moral standards." There seems to be nothing in that list that the American Civil Liberties Union would oppose.

The second action urged by our former U.S. attorney general is: "If you know of any left-wing actions or policies (campus outrages) at your alma mater or at colleges and universities in your area, please include them here," and space is provided. If more space is needed or you would like to talk to someone personally "about campus outrages," you can contact Chad Kifer at 1-800-526-7022 or ckifer@isi.org.

I doubt that the "campus outrages" Ashcroft and his colleagues at the ISI are interested in hearing about would include, for instance, the fact that many of our large universities pay their football coach salaries in the millions of dollars while elementary schoolteachers in the same area are fortunate to make enough money to raise a family.

The real intent of the letter is to set citizens to spying on other citizens—à la Joe McCarthy—whom they don't agree with, whose politics or religion are different from theirs. The purpose of this encouragement to report on those who don't conform to your beliefs is to drive deeper the religious/political wedges that divide us and turn neighbor against neighbor in an escalation of suspicion, hatred, and fear.

† † †

It's Thanksgiving Sunday of 2004, and the altar of my church is decorated with a cornucopia, symbolizing the bounty of the season, the blessing of the harvest. Our minister, the Reverend Donna Schaper, a dark-haired, passionate preacher who paces the altar with a handheld microphone rather than reading behind a pulpit, is also decorated for the occasion, wearing, in the church's tradition, a baggy brown pilgrim's outfit with white hat and collar. The costume makes her feel ridiculous, not to speak of hot in the eighty-degrees-plus weather of Miami that day. She starts off comforting the congregation with holiday-appropriate stories of the feast of everyday life, the delight in festive meals with friends and family, but then her sermon takes a darker turn.

"I promised the church council I wouldn't preach about politics today, because of the holiday," she says, "but I'm afraid I can't keep my promise."

A sudden quiet, almost a pall, comes over the congregation.

Like most mainline Protestant churches today in America, ours is divided by those who want to come to church just to feel good about themselves and be reassured by their faith without the disturbance of events in the world around them, and those who come to church to learn how their faith is related to those troubling events and how we can try to apply our belief to our daily life.

Our minister tells the congregation about events leading up to the previous day's demonstration here to protest the meeting of the FTAA (the Free Trade Area of the Americas, an attempted expansion of NAFTA to Central and South America). The church had accepted a request by our national denomination, the United Church of Christ (UCC, known as the most liberal mainline denomination along with the Unitarian-Universalist Association) to play host to a hundred UCC demonstrators coming from around the country to join the protest.

A conservative member of the church council, disgruntled by

the plan to host out-of-town protestors, reported it to the local police department, and a sergeant was dispatched to tell the minister and her staff they shouldn't do this. The sergeant lectured the ministers that when he was a boy, the youth at his church were taught to read the Bible, not to protest.

The sergeant's sermonette was followed up by a letter from the city manager suggesting the church would be out of compliance with zoning laws if they provided shelter for their denominational brethren and sisters from out of town, noting that "You are not a hotel." Since the church is in the process of applying for precious zoning permits for an addition to the overcrowded Sunday School building, the tension is great. A compromise is reached when the fifty-seven guests who arrive on an overnight bus are housed in church members' homes rather than on sleeping bags and blankets on the floor of the church's Fellowship Hall.

Reverend Donna breaks her promise not to talk about politics from the pulpit to tell the congregation she went to the demonstration the day before and feels the Miami police "ridiculously overreacted with force," spending $18.5 million to come out in full riot gear, and:

> unnecessarily used rubber bullets on demonstrators, attacked two press photographers and destroyed their camera equipment, and shot a rubber bullet in the eye of a reporter. The chief of police swore at demonstrators while egging on his troops with such patriotic exhortations as "Those pussies will be destroyed at the end of the day."

Cattle prods, electric wands, pepper spray, and other crowd control measures were used, and young demonstrators were herded off to jail as part of what Donna feels is an unnecessary use of force. "This country," Reverend Schaper says, "may be in the same early stages as Germany during the rise of Nazism."

The hush that comes over the congregation is broken by an angry voice that rises from a little over halfway back in the church.

"I will not sit here and listen to this," shouts a middle-aged man who has risen from his pew to interrupt the sermon. All eyes of more than four hundred worshippers turn to see an apparently middle-class, properly dressed citizen who has just broken the most basic protocol of church behavior. I have attended Protestant services off and on for the last fifty years and this is the first time I have ever heard someone in a congregation rise to interrupt a sermon.

"I believe George Bush is a great president," the man announces, "and besides that, my wife was almost hit by a brick thrown by one of the demonstrators." (He later admits to the minister that this wasn't true but it heightens the drama.)

Reverend Donna keeps her cool, saying in a calm, steady voice that she is glad he feels he is free to speak out like this and she would welcome a chance to discuss his views further if he comes to her office. (She has two conversations with him later and learns he is a doctor and is not a member of the church.)

A few more ranting shouts, though, and the man leaves. Donna returns to the altar, continues the service with dignity, and all stand and sing the closing hymn. Donna's husband, history professor and author Warren Goldstein, rushes up to give her a hug as other friends and supporters gather around. She rests for a moment, trembling a little, in Warren's embrace, then gathers herself and hurries to her duty at the main entrance to shake hands and exchange greetings with departing worshippers.

Many of the congregants are supportive and sympathetic as they leave, while some express their anger. One church council member who has made it clear she doesn't like controversy in church departs without speaking, joining her fellow wor-shipper who interrupted the service. A member who had signed a petition criticizing Donna's ministry complains as she leaves that the critics had specifically asked her "not to preach politics from the pulpit." A worshipper whom Donna has seen before stops on his way out and says to Reverend Schaper "Come close"; as she bends her head near to him, he whispers "You hypocrite," and spits on her neck.

Onward, Christian soldiers.

The following summer, Donna resigns as minister after five years in the post, citing her professor husband's inability to find the kind of faculty position he had hoped for in South Florida, which necessitated commuting to Connecticut, where he serves as professor of history at the University of Hartford. Reverend Donna Schaper signs on as pastor of a small church in North Hadley, Massachusetts, but leaves that position in less than a year and is working for the United Church of Christ national campaign God Is Still Speaking ("Still Speaking Initiative"), promoting the denomination and making its principles known to the public at large.

† † †

Joseph Hough Jr., president of Union Theological Seminary, says, as he speaks about the influence of the Religious Right: "Sometimes I think this is more dangerous to democracy than anything I've seen in my lifetime."

The stately towers of Union Theological Seminary, which rise above upper Broadway on Manhattan's West Side, were once the symbol of "the stronghold of liberal Christianity in America" in the days when Reinhold Niebuhr held forth in the seminary's classrooms. Not only was Niebuhr the leading Protestant theologian of the era, he was also a social activist who wrote for *The Nation* as well as Christian magazines and founded the liberal Americans for Democratic Action. Today Union Seminary seems more the embattled fortress of a main-line Protestantism in decline whose membership rolls and influence drain away each year.

"Union is a shadow now of what it once was," I am told by Scott Harshbarger, an advisor to the president of Union Theological Seminary. "They raised money and brought in Joseph Hough Jr. as president," Harshbarger continues. "A friend of mine said 'Now that we've got the money, we need the passion and energy.' Getting Joe, anyway, was a step in the right direction."

Dr. Hough, former dean and professor of ethics at Vanderbilt University Divinity School, is a balding man with a white mustache and a gentleman's old-fashioned warmth of personality. He speaks in a soft Southern accent as he tells me, "Public policy is now presented in religious terms. We have the most explosive framing of political discourse in the history of this country—brilliantly done, ruthlessly done—so that suddenly a man's qualification for office doesn't have anything to do with his program unless it conforms to the Religious Right's moral issues."

Dr. Hough shakes his head in frustration and sorrow.

"People who voted that way," he said, "believed they were voting for God."

† † †

In an office tower overlooking Boston Harbor sits Scott Harshbarger, former attorney general of Massachusetts, past president of Common Cause, and former Democratic candidate for governor, who went to Union on a Rockefeller grant and served an internship with the East Harlem Protestant Parish before choosing law over ministry. A broad-shouldered, thick-chested man, Harshbarger has maintained the physique of a firststringer on the Harvard football team of 1964 and exudes a restless energy. In his role as advisor to the president of Union, he hopes to help make the seminary the kind of force it once was in the life of liberal religion in America.

"The Religious Right has co-opted the terms 'Christianity' and 'Jesus Christ,'" Harshbarger says, "or 'hijacked them,' as a lot of people put it now. But 'hijacking' isn't quite right, because *it was done in the broad light of day*. It was taken right away from us and we let it happen."

Hijacking Jesus was so easily accomplished that the Religious Right, while they are at it, are now scooping up Buddha, Mohammed, Moses, and any other available divines, claiming them and their followers for the cause. Senator Bill Frist first upped the ante in his *Justice Sunday* television show when he tried to use God to rally support for President Bush's 2005 slate of conservative judicial nominees. With a straight face, Frist told a national TV audience that a vote against Bush's right-wing judges is a vote against "people of faith," thus appointing himself the spokesman not only for Christians but also Jews, Muslims, Mormons, Hindus, Buddhists, and Sikhs. Senator Frist and his militant "Christian Soldiers" are claiming new spiritual territory with the zeal of Hitler's Panzer divisions overrunning Poland. Robert Edgar, general secretary of the National Council of Churches, points out that "It's not just Christians they're isolating—it's anybody who's different from them—they have the direct line to God."

Senator Ken Salazar of Colorado incurred the wrath of the Right Religionists for being one of the nonpartisan group of fourteen senators who broke the deadlock on Bush's judicial appointments with a compromise that stopped the Republicans' "nuclear option" from blowing up the Senate rules that allow the filibuster.

Focus on the Family, the powerful right-wing group headed by James Dobson and headquartered in Colorado Springs, "vilified" Salazar, he says, because of his role in the Senate compromise. Salazar charged on Colorado Public Radio that "the tactics and the agenda of the Religious Right is in fact an un-Christian agenda. . . . They are hijacking Christianity for political purposes." Claiming that his own family's roots in Christianity go back to "the Stone Age," the senator said on the program *Colorado Matters* that the Religious Right, in the name of Christianity, "has become an appendage of the right wing of the Republican Party."

Political science professor Kenneth Wald of the University of Florida puts it in an even more concrete way: "The Religious Right has been institutionalized within the Republican Party."

Did it happen when no one was looking?

I decide to go to Washington to find some answers.

† † †

A direct route from the front door of the White House leads across Lafayette Square to a the door of an impressive, high-spired, yellow-bright building with six white stone pillars and a plaque at the entrance denoting it as a registered national historical landmark. This is St. John's Episcopal Church, where "Every United States president since James Madison has attended services," according to a plaque by the door—including George W. Bush.

The Rev. Spencer Rice, a priest-in-residence at St. John's, tells me:

> It's absolutely true that in the public mind the term "Christian" has come to mean Fundamentalist or Evangelical. In my public talks, I seldom if ever use the term "Christianity" anymore. I find myself preaching much more about Jesus than about Christ because everything is so loaded now. I think people feel a commonality with Jesus—who he was, what he stood for, what he passed on to generations is something valuable. When you say Jesus *the Christ* [which means he is not only human but also divine]—boy, that's loaded.

Rev. Rice, who is semiretired after a distinguished national career in his denomination, is a tall, courtly, white-haired man in a crisp white shirt, dark-red tie, and black suit, who has the manner and air of an ambassador. A lifelong Republican, he was "social friends with George '41' and Barbara," and when he was a pastor in San Francisco and Ronald Reagan was governor of California, "I said the invocation for Reagan on many occasions."

"Reagan pulled the conservative religious people along," he continues:

> but he was not captured by them. President Bush '42,' is another bag of cats. I am very fond of him as a person—he was here on Sunday—he's here every Sunday he's in town. Everybody says he's Fundamentalist—no doubt about it, that was his conversion. But I have no idea whether he conveyed this religious emphasis to his staff or whether the Rove types, who understand America, seized upon this for pragmatic reasons rather than religious reasons. It's probably both. I'm confident that helped him dramatically in the election. To what extent it's accurate I can't testify. He allowed his public religious image to be part of the campaign. He likes to come to the eight o'clock service because he says it's "more Biblical."

† † †

In the last presidential election, white Evangelicals made up 23 percent of the population, 37 percent of the Republican Party, and gave George W. Bush 78 percent of their vote, according to

the Pew Research Center. Todd M. Johnson, director of the
Center for the Study of Global Christianity at the conservative
Gordon–Conwell Theological Seminary, distributed statistics
and graphs at a conference of the National Association of Evangelicals showing that U.S. Evangelicals totaled 44 million,
making up 22.6 percent of the population.

Many more Americans than those who consider themselves
Evangelicals or "born again" Christians are influenced by the
overwhelming voice of Religious Right radio, television, and
press. The Barna Group of researchers conducted a nationwide
survey showing that in a typical month more than half the
nation's adults had listened to a Christian radio station, 43 percent had watched Christian programming on television, and
one out of every three adults claimed to have read a Christian
book other than the Bible.

The National Religious Broadcasters group has more than
sixteen hundred member stations and calls itself "your partner
to promote the Gospel." The overwhelming majority of this
Christian media transmits the messages of the Religious Right,
like the TV shows of Pat Robertson, Jerry Falwell, and James
M. Kennedy. The radio commentaries of Focus on the Family's
James C. Dobson alone are heard by more than two hundred
million people every day in ninety-nine countries on more than
five thousand radio outlets.

Topping all books on the national bestseller charts is the Left
Behind series, with eleven installments and more on the way,
totaling sixty million in sales at latest reckoning. More Americans
have read these books than the works of John Grisham and
Anne Rice put together. They are created by the team of Tim

LeHaye, a leading theologian of the Religious Right, with the aid of ghostwriter Jerry B. Jenkins. (Jenkins's "as-told-to" subjects range from evangelist Billy Graham to knuckleball pitcher Nolan Ryan.) These theological thrillers are dramatizations purporting to show that the Bible has foretold the current world crisis that is leading to the apocalyptic "end times" and the Second Coming of Christ.

The Left Behind books are based on the beliefs of the Dispensationalists, a powerful Religious Right faction that believes Bush's foreign policy in the Middle East—featuring the invasion of Iraq—is following biblical prophecy that will lead to Armageddon and the "end times" of the world. To the Dispensationalists this shows that Bush and his policies are part of the Divine Plan, while to those who hope the world is still around for their children and grandchildren, the plan doesn't look so divine.

In the world according to LeHaye and the Dispensationalists, the beginning of the end of the world will be "the Rapture," when the Christians who are "saved" are snatched out of their shoes and beamed up to heaven. This event is dramatized in the first of the Left Behind books when a flight attendant on an airborne plane finds about half the seats that were occupied only a moment before are empty except for the suits, dresses, jewelry, and watches of passengers taken up in what might be thought of by non-Dispensationalists as the Big Snatch.

The "Left Behind" of the title, by the way, does not refer to the discarded clothing of the passengers, but the wives, husbands, and children who were not among the "saved" and so must remain on earth to battle the Antichrist (who, of course, in these fictions is a liberal leader of the United Nations). If they endure Armageddon, as well as the floods, diseases, and plagues of the time of Tribulation that ensues, the good guys who were left behind will be rewarded by the Second Coming of Christ and his thousand-year reign on earth.

This epic, which is wilder than Dungeons and Dragons, more bizarre than anything dreamed up by Isaac Asimov, was culled from the Old Testament Prophets and the Book of Revelation, which predicts the end times and the Second Coming of Christ. Although the word "Rapture" does not actually appear in the Book of Revelation, the clever Dispensationalists have discerned that it's really there *in code*. Of such material was this fantasy structure tacked together by an English pastor in the late 1850s.

Who could have imagined that such a system would capture the fancy of millions of citizens of the most powerful country in the world in the twenty-first century? Yet American motorists seem to know the meaning of the bumper sticker that says "This Car Will Have No Driver if the Rapture Occurs." To insure the continued popularity of this fantasy (and indoctrination of a new generation) there is a Left Behind: The Kids series for youth from ages ten to fourteen that tells the story (in more than thirty volumes) of four teenagers who are left behind after the Rapture and join forces in the fight against Satan.

Theological theories spun from such scriptural contortions abound on the Religious Right. Dispensationalists include the "Premillennialists" who believe Jesus will come before Armageddon and be on earth to preside over the thousand-year reign of peace, as well as "Postmillennialists" who believe the

thousand years of peace is the reign of the *Church* on earth and
Jesus will come *after* it. The "Preemies" are the Christians who
support Israel, believing it must remain as a state for the biblical
prophesies of Revelation to come true, while the "Posties" don't
care if Israel is around or not, since Jesus won't be returning
until after the thousand-year reign of peace.

The oddball theories, ideas, and rationales of Dispensationalism reach and influence the president of the United States.
Tony Campolo, a well-known progressive Evangelical author
(*Following Jesus without Embarrassing God*), and professor
emeritus of sociology at Eastern University, tells me that "I
know Franklin Graham [the son and heir apparent of Billy]
would fall into that category—Dispensationalism—and I know
he's close to the president. Falwell is a Dispensationalist and so
is Robertson, and insofar as George W. Bush is giving them his
ear—and he *is*—he's really listening to these people."

The "Dispensationalists" believe that history is divided into
different "dispensations," or eras, of God, and that in the current "dispensation" we are living in, the "Sermon on the
Mount" does not apply. This is one of the most eloquent and
well-known teachings of Jesus, composed of the series of "blessings" he gives to the multitudes on the mountain, including
"Blessed are the meek," and "Blessed are the peacemakers."
Those blessings mean help for the downtrodden and are
against war, so they obviously don't fit the creed of the Religious Right.

The rhetoric of the Religious Right has turned Jesus into a
symbol of Christian jihad or, in line with the Bush administration's vision, commander of the Crusades in a nuclear age.

President Bush early on christened the war against terrorism a "crusade," which is part of his justification for invading and attempting to "convert" the Middle East to democracy, which goes hand in hand with the Religious Right's dream of converting the region—and eventually the world—to Christianity. This method of "conversion" is brought about not by spiritual transformation but by military force (the kind of conversion one U.S. Army chaplain conducted by forcing his troops to be baptized before getting a bath).

An unexpected key to understanding the administration's blend of Republican foreign policy and right-wing Christian theology came to me during a talk with William F. Buckley Jr., whom I first interviewed for a profile in *Esquire* magazine a few years after he founded the *National Review* in New York in the fifties. During many other interviews over the ensuing decades, I have always found Mr. Buckley to be as honestly frank and straightforward in his responses as he is reliably to the right in his politics (with occasional surprises in political opinions, such as his support for the legalization of drugs in the United States, that I'll bet the gambling moralist William Bennett would have never taken odds on during his frequent trips to Vegas).

I had sensed in a TV interview shortly after the invasion of Iraq that Buckley seemed less than enthusiastic about that undertaking than his conservative Republican comrades. When I ask him, during an interview at his home in New York, his feelings about going into Iraq, Buckley responds that "I found it more problematic than the neocons do. To the extent that the war in Iraq is identified with politics, it's the Jewish neocons who were the principal animators."

He goes on to say "It's sad that some people who really should confess the [Christian] faith can't do it because of pride. Or so it strikes me. Podhoretz, Kristol—they want to become Christians. Remember Willie Schlamm years ago? He said he'd be a Christian tomorrow—but 'I can't do that to my [Jewish] faith.'"

Who besides Bill Buckley, who knows these men, could have guessed that the neocons are closet Christians? If they are also "closet Dispensationalists," it would help explain the neocon obsession with the Middle East and the administration's policy of trying to control that part of the world. It fits right in with the Religious Right's plan for religious apocalypse and the "end-times" strategy. Wacky as that may sound, there is nothing wackier than the religious-political roots of George W. Bush's invasion of Iraq and the U.S. Middle East policy that smells of Christian jihad.

Christian mission campaigns sponsored by some Evangelical churches are focusing on "the spirit of Babylon" (Iraq) and "the Prince of Persia" (Iran) in the belief that these areas must be "penetrated" by Christianity. In an article in *Sojourners* magazine called "Praise the Lord and Pass the Ammunition," Josh Anderson charged that "President Bush has repeatedly adorned his foreign policy with strong evangelical overtones [so that] wars conducted against nation-states threaten to link seamlessly with the spiritual battles that missionaries have been engaged in for centuries."

In an example of the synergy of the Religious Right with the Bush administration, the Associated Press reported that the Southern Baptist Convention not only sent missionaries into

Iraq in late 2003 but before that had helped draft a letter that urged Bush to attack that country.

Some Religious Right zealots see missionary work as an arm of the U.S. armed forces. John F. Sugg, an award-winning investigative reporter who has written for the *Miami Herald*, the *Atlanta Constitution*, and the *American Lawyer*, told a conference on the Religious Right at New York University that Rev. Charles Stanley of Atlanta, a former president of the Southern Baptist Convention, wanted to dispatch his missionaries alongside American troops in Iraq. Rev. Stanley proclaimed that "God favors war for divine reasons and sometimes uses it to accomplish his will."

That message hardly seems to fit with Jesus' teaching to "Love your enemies, bless them that curse you, do good to them that hate you, and pray for them which despitefully use you, and persecute you."

† † †

The shock of 9/11 has stimulated the search of Americans for answers, reassurance, comfort, and security, and many people look to religion to satisfy those desires. In such times of uncertainty, those who most loudly and dogmatically trumpet the Truth as their exclusive domain and paint the world in clearest hues of good and evil seem most appealing.

"Before 9/11, the power of the Evangelicals within the mainline churches was waning," says Jan Love, head of the Women's Division of the United Methodist Church. "But afterward there was a sharp consolidation of the right in the United States—the

Cultural Right, the Political Right, and the Religious Right. That consolidation gave the Evangelicals a new boost. It gave them momentum."

Senator Richard Lugar (R-Ind.), chairman of the Senate Foreign Relations Committee, tells me:

Since 9/11 there's been a very different atmosphere and concern in this country—people started thinking about the end of their lives, about ultimate questions, and that may be responsible for the intensity of religious interest. These things do affect our spirituality —people taking things seriously, going back to their roots. We go through these phases in our history. We've had "religious awakenings" before—then there are other times when we're not so worried about the world. This may be a kind of cyclical thing; but for the moment we're going to be in some sense of urgency.

Lugar has thick white hair and deep, dark circles under his eyes, earned from the arduous multidecade task of serving as a voice of balance and sanity within his party (highlighted by his leading an American delegation to observe the 1986 Philippine Presidential Election, announcing that the election was fatally flawed by wholesale fraud and abuse, and then persuading President Ronald Reagan to ask President Ferdinand Marcos to step down in favor of the legitimate winner, Corazon Aquino). Lugar started his career on the Indianapolis School Board during a difficult period of school integration and was elected mayor in November 1967, just months before the assassination of Dr. Martin Luther King Jr. on April 4, 1968:

My involvement with African-Americans became very intense—I was literally in church basements and pulpits wherever I could talk to people who were African-American, and miraculously we escaped wholesale disorder, which was remarkable in light of what was going on all around us. It came from the religious community acting in a very different way than is being suggested now.

I don't dispute the importance of turnouts that may have come from this energy [of the Religious Right] because I think it was for real, and more Republicans voted than ever before. Since the 2004 election the Evangelicals say "Listen, we were the reason you won, and now we want more attention—to *our* issues." And they're saying this at the state houses, at the city halls, and in Congress. We have a bill on the floor today that deals with bankruptcy, and some of them said, "Well, that's all very interesting, but that's more of a warmed-over commercial agenda, of business groups. And we haven't yet seen the sorts of things that were pivotal to the election."

You don't have to be a political analyst to know what they mean. Abortion. Gay marriage. Gay rights.

Dick Lugar is a formal man with a wry wit; looking back at the last presidential election, he says with a kind of bemused wonder, "There was not really an appeal of either party to so-called 'moderates,' to Independents—almost a lack of recognition that such people may *exist* in this world!"

† † †

Orwell, thou shouldst be living at this hour! Ahead of his time as always, the great English author George Orwell was simply twenty years too soon in picking 1984 as the date in which he set his novel of a world in which a Big Brother government turns words into their opposite meanings—Peace means War, Love means Hate, Dark means Light. Several years after the president declared "Mission Accomplished" in Iraq, and as it rages on more fiercely than ever, it is declared no longer a "war" but rather a "struggle" against world terrorism. As Air America radio's Randi Rhodes commented, a "struggle" might be more accurately defined as Paris Hilton having difficulty carrying all her purchases to her car after shopping at the mall.

In our topsy-turvy society, the leaders of the Religious Right are more open and aggressive in using the terminology of war than are their political counterparts; these ministers who are more comfortable with the rhetoric of battle than are senators and generals. Jerry Falwell assures the faithful that "God is Prowar." Recruiters of the Religious Right are enlisting "soldiers" and "warriors" to the ranks of their "army." Their language is military, from the World Prayer Center at Colorado Springs, which is proudly known as "a spiritual NORAD" to the "Commanders" of the Royal Rangers, the Religious Right version of the Boy Scouts, whose training for manhood includes pistol, shotgun, and muzzle-loading rifle training, beginning in the "subjunior" category of ages eleven to thirteen, and a merit badge in "atomic energy," which requires constructing "a Bohr model of the Hydrogen Atom model of the atom."

General William Boykin, a professional Army man, is part of a group that applies military principles to evangelism, rallying troops to "the spiritual warfare for souls." He preaches to crowds across the country that America is a "Christian nation" engaged in a holy war against Satan and that the only way to defeat the Muslim enemies is to "come against them in the name of Jesus." Though officers at the Air Force Academy have been warned not to evangelize, evidently the Army—or at least Boykin—is exempt from such strictures; he was rewarded with the post of deputy undersecretary of defense for Intelligence.

Bill Bright, founder and head of the Campus Crusade for Christ International, in a foreword to *The Gates of Hell Shall Not Prevail* by megachurch pastor and Religious Right televangelist James Kennedy, prayed that God use Kennedy and his book "to help mobilize citizens of this country and particularly the body of Christ, God's army, in this crucial, historic hour. Now is the time for action!"

Rev. Kennedy endorses Gary North, a leader of the ultra-right Reconstructionist movement, who wrote that "In winning a nation to the Gospel, the sword as well as the pen must be used." The nation he's talking about is not Iraq but the United States. His movement's goal is to turn America into a Christian theocracy. For those who disobey God's law (as interpreted by the movement's leaders) Mr. North (as well as his fellow Reconstructionists) advocates stoning, because rocks are "cheap" and "plentiful."

This movement is also known as Theonomy ("The Rule of God") and Dominion Theology, based on God's directive in Genesis to the humans he had just created to "subdue" the earth and to "have dominion . . . over every living thing that moveth upon the earth." That means you, brother and sister, if you don't believe as they do, and under their rule the death penalty would be administered for homosexuality, adultery, and blasphemy (this is where the stoning comes in). Although this is a fringe movement, its books and ideas have influenced national Evangelical leaders, including Jerry Falwell and D. James Kennedy, an original board member of the Moral Majority, pastor of a megachurch in Ft. Lauderdale, Florida, and a popular purveyor of militant religion through a TV and radio ministry that reaches throughout the nation.

Dr. Kennedy wrote the foreword to a book called *The Changing of the Guard: The Vital Role Christians Must Play in America's Unfolding Political and Cultural Drama*, in which he praised its author, the Evangelical activist and educator George Grant, for urging Christian soldiers "to contend for the faith in the political arena as devotedly as the early martyrs were forced to contend in physical arenas." Modern martyrs are needed to fight for the right, Kennedy explained, because "every evil and injustice known to humanity is coming out of the closet and parading down Main Street." These martyrs must battle the evil opponents who "rattle their sabers against the people of God," according to Grant; his "saber-wielders" include the Children's Defense Fund, the National Organization for Women, the American Civil Liberties Union, People for the American Way, Greenpeace, and the World Health Organization.

Most of those groups as well as their millions of sympathizers and supporters believe in human rights for all, but Religious Right author Grant does not. He explained:

> The Bible does not guarantee human rights. At the time of the
> fall, man lost all rights except the right to die. . . . What this means
> is that all protection, all justice, all compassion, and all fairness
> are given to men on the basis of grace, and an adherence to the
> Scriptures, not on some nebulous and subjective notion of rights.

Megachurch pastor Kennedy, in his book *The Gates of Hell
Shall Prevail: The Attack on Christianity and What You Need to
Know to Combat It*, predicted that "If either of our major political parties wakes up and smells the coffee, understands the
signs of the times, perceives what is happening, and embraces
the moral biblical agenda of Christians . . . that party will be in
power for the next century."

When that was written a decade ago, in 1996, it would have
seemed like a pipe dream of conservative Evangelicals and
Fundamentalists. After the last two national elections and the
burgeoning power of the Religious Right, it sounds like an all-
too-plausible nightmare for the rest of us.

† † †

The ascendancy of the spirit of violence, prejudice, and rage as
symbols of religion in this society is perhaps epitomized in the
bloodbath of Mel Gibson's masochistic movie *The Passion of the
Christ*, which is surely spawning anti-Semitism and crusader-
shrouded militarism in generations to come. Millions of words
have already been written in criticism, complaint, defense, and
adoration of the film—though not as many millions of words
may have been written about it as millions of dollars have been

and will be made on it—and people worldwide have chosen sides with or without seeing the bloody blockbuster.

At first I avoided seeing it, after Professor Harvey Cox, the Harvard theologian and author, told me he had walked out after the scene where Jesus was hung over a bridge upside down, which was nothing like he—nor anyone else—had read in the Gospels or anywhere else in the Bible.

A Boston TV station rounding up religious authorities to discuss *The Passion of the Christ* called Rabbi Harold Kushner, author of bestsellers such as *When Bad Things Happen to Good People*, and asked if he had seen the movie. "No," he told them, "but I've read the book," and declined their invitation to participate in their discussion.

I too had "read the book"—which I assumed was the New Testament, or anyway the Gospels of Matthew, Mark, Luke, and John, which purport to tell the story of the life and death of Jesus. This did not prepare me for the movie. In "the book"— or the books—there is no attractive female figure of evil with a snake under her garment who slithers out to strike at Jesus before his arrest in the Garden of Gethsemane—"Evil takes on the form of beauty" Gibson helpfully explained at a pastors' screening according to *Christianity Today*. My favorite addition to what once used to be called "The Greatest Story Ever Told"—before Mel Gibson got a hold of it—was the flashback where Jesus is working at home as a carpenter and his mother shakes her head at some newfangled kind of table he has just made and hopes to sell to a rich man. "It'll never catch on," she tells him.

Such comic relief is rare, however, for most of the movie is a pornographic masochist's dream of the scourging, lashing, and torture of a blood-soaked, flesh-ripped Jesus that makes Cronenberg's *The History of Violence* look like a feature for *Sesame Street*. The real message, however, comes in the chilling manner in which, after Jesus is entombed and the tomb is closed, his resurrection is represented by a "before" image of Jesus without the blood, looking strong, healthy, determined, ready to roll, and in the background, the rising beat of a military march with drums. This gives the militant ranks of the Religious Right their theme song—no words, just drumbeats, growing louder.

II.

Earthly Revelation: Evangelicals Discover Blacks, the Poor, and the Environment!

One of the principal battalions of the Armies of the Right is trying to hold its ranks together. Before Jim Wallis and his best-selling book *God's Politics*, came along, the media and the populace at large thought that all Evangelicals were soldiers of the Right. It was not widely known that the National Association of Evangelicals (NAE) is not the monolithic force it pretends to be, and that in fact it has its own political left flank.

I first got a hint of this when a friend sent me a clipping from the *Boston Globe* with the headline: "Official Chides Christian Right; Moral Majority Called Aberration."

The shocking part of the article was not that such charges

were made but that they were made by a "top official" of the
NAE. Robert Wenz, vice president for national ministries of
the NAE, held a press conference at Gordon–Cromwell Theological Seminary and told a group of reporters that although the
Evangelicals were enjoying greater cultural influence due to
their newfound electoral clout, they had sometimes "lost their
perspective" by forgetting about issues like poverty and the
environment.

Dr. Wenz, who seemed to be temporarily channeling Bill
Moyers, declared that the "Moral Majority" phenomenon that
pumped up the Religious Right in the eighties was "an aberration, and a regrettable one at that," for even though it got
Evangelicals into the political process, Jerry Falwell's organization was "fatally flawed by a hubris that made the movement
condescending and more than a bit judgmental."

It sounded as if the Evangelical leader was speaking in
tongues of liberal fire. Was he cribbing from the sermons of
William Sloane Coffin? It sounded like it when Rev. Wenz
declared "The Moral Majority lacked a servant heart of Christ
born out of humility and compassion for a fallen humanity.
Instead, it was about making America a nice place for Christians to live. This is not the kind of social involvement that we
need."

Further shock lay ahead when the *Globe* reported that Dr.
Wenz said it was important that Evangelicals be clear that they
have no allegiance to the Republican Party and that the GOP
owes them nothing. If Ralph Reed and Karl Rove read this
article—much less Jerry Falwell and Pat Robertson—they all
must have grabbed their Bromo Seltzer.

The Globe article said that this event was the first of a series of conferences at which Evangelicals would attempt to explain their faith to reporters and answer questions. I immediately went to my computer, found the NAE Web site, and signed up for the next conference, to be held in Washington, D.C. Then I sent an e-mail to Dr. Wenz, saying how much I admired the sentiments he expressed as reported in the *Globe* article and asking if I could interview him at the Washington conference.

Dr. Wenz e-mailed back: "Thanks, Dan, for the kind words. Not everyone liked the report in the *Globe*! I'd be happy to meet with you on Thursday the tenth for as long as you might need."

I was pleased and excited, both as a reporter and a Christian. It sounded as if Dr. Wenz's words might signal a transformation of the Evangelical vanguard from the Warrior Christ back to the values of the Jesus of the Sermon on the Mount; and if that were true, Robert Wenz and his message would be a major story in the national influence of the Religious Right—religiously, politically, and socially.

My grand illusion ended with almost the first words spoken by Dr. Wenz at the Washington conference. "I was misquoted," he told the NAE audience, referring to the *Boston Globe* article, "and my words were taken out of context."

When he'd answered my e-mail of praise after reading the *Globe* article and thanked me "for the kind words," he made no mention of his own words being misquoted or taken out of context. When he said in that e-mail, "Not everyone liked the report in the *Globe*," there must have been such an outpouring of opposition from his fellow Evangelicals that by the time of the Washington conference a month later he had to dissociate himself from what seemed to be his own genuine sentiments of humility, repentance, and political independence.

None of this means that Robert Wenz is a liar or that the *Globe* reporter was trying unfairly to cast him as a reincarnation of Reinhold Niebuhr, the great liberal theologian. What it means is that some of the NAE leadership is embarrassed by Pat Robertson and Jerry Falwell, but they can't be critical of them because they would alienate their own base. They are trying to appease the growing group of their colleagues who believe in some of the principle issues Jesus addressed—primarily, poverty and peace—and still hold on to those who follow the ethics of Robertson, Falwell, and the Bush administration's economic policies that favor the rich, reduce the middle class, and squeeze the poor, as well as its policies for war, adding Pat Robertson's ingenious suggestion to avoid war in Venezuela by assassinating its president.

Robert Wenz welcomed the assembled guests "to this briefing, symposium, seminar, whatever word you'd like" at the National Press Club in Washington, a venue denoting the Evangelicals' cultural promotion, thanks to their political clout, from the boondocks to the Beltway.

"Dr. Bob"—as Wenz identifies himself in his e-mail—is not at all the gregarious "Dr. Phil"–type nor the Bible-thumping, hollering Swaggart sort, but a rather mild-mannered, polite, low-key kind of man, one you might guess to be an academic, which he is as well as being a preacher. A balding man of average size in a brown suit, white shirt, and dark-red tie, he reminded me of Dean Rusk, though I doubt he'd want to be identified with President John F. Kennedy's secretary of state. Holman Lounge, the room where the conference was held at the National Press Club, indeed might have been mistaken for the scene of a State Department press briefing—gray, anonymous, high-ceilinged, drained of personality, with a speaker's podium and raised platform at the front and a backdrop of long, whitish-gray draperies from behind which might have emerged the ghost of some nameless bureaucrat. No decoration to relieve the eye interrupted the pale stretches of blank walls, no hint, trace, or whiff of any sight or substance suggestive of the subject of the gathering.

The Evangelicals, presenting their new image of enlightened awareness of centuries-old issues, had established an aura of purest objectivity. Like Dr. Wenz, the speakers here were scholarly (most, in fact, were academics), low-key, and as passionless in their delivery as the colorless cast of the room (with the exception of an African-American minister who brought some life to the afternoon as he recounted the racist history of his hosts' movement). These NAE officials are for the most part the movements' more mainstream intellectuals and leaders, just as the magazine *Christianity Today*, founded by Billy Graham, positions itself at the center of the Evangelical press (it is journalistically sound and feisty and is not afraid to editorialize against NAE positions).

As they signed in, guests from the media who had previously registered for the event online and been approved were given a media guide titled *What Is an Evangelical? A Seminar for Media Professionals*. This document supplied background material on the speakers as well as a "Statement of Faith" that began with the belief that the Bible is "the inspired, the only infallible, authoritative Word of God," and included a principle that may have given momentary hope and then snatched it back from those notoriously atheistic members of the press: "We believe in the resurrection of both the saved and the lost; they that are saved unto the resurrection of life and they that are damned, lost unto the resurrection of damnation."

Perhaps as solace, at least for the afternoon, the saved (presumably including representatives of Evangelical publications) and the lost alike were offered a choice of coffee, Coke, or springwater and an oatmeal cookie before taking a seat at one of the white-cloth-covered tables arrayed before the podium. A scattering of twenty or so media people, mixed in with Evangelical speakers and officials, were dotted around the room as Dr. Wenz gave his opening remarks.

"We want to help you understand who Evangelicals are," he explained:

> There's some misunderstanding, because it's very difficult at times to explain or define what Evangelical is. We represent different traditions—three of us are Episcopalians, we have a Pentecostal minister, a Congregationalist, I'm from the Christian Missionary Alliance, and we have a wide spectrum of Evangelical voices here. We want to present to you here what it means in twenty-first-century America to be an Evangelical.

An Evangelical press representative who wanted some clarification held up his hand and said:

David Brooks in the *New York Times* wrote about the misunderstanding about Evangelicals. He wrote that there's a major difference between people of faith and the made-for-TV Elmer Gantry–style blowhards who are selected to represent them. Falwell and Pat Robertson are held up as spokesmen for Evangelicals, which is ridiculous. Meanwhile, people like the theologian John Stott who are actually important get ignored. How do you respond to that?"

After his comment reported in the *Globe* that Falwell's Moral Majority was a regrettable aberration fatally flawed by hubris, I wondered how he'd respond now among his fellow Evangelicals.

"We like Pat Robertson and we love Jerry Falwell as men who are deeply committed men of God," Dr. Wenz replied.

"But are they accurate spokesmen for Evangelicals?" the questioner pursued.

"We are dealing with a media world," Dr. Wenz hedged:

and in that world the voices don't come from being elected but from having access to the media. Pat Robertson has his own television network, and Jerry Falwell has had significant access to the media for the past twenty-five years. Ted Haggard [president of the NAE] was elected by a body of thirty million people, and we would encourage you to talk with him if you really want to find out what Evangelicals are thinking.

While promoting the president of the NAE as the *elected* spokesman for the Evangelicals, neither Dr. Wenz nor any other speaker had anything negative to say about Jerry Falwell, Pat Robertson, or the Moral Majority for the rest of the day— nor did Dr. Wenz or anyone else suggest the Evangelicals had "lost their perspective" after their newfound power at the polls.

That power, in fact, had just been demonstrated at the luncheon before the conference when a U.S. senator from each party showed up to pay obeisance to the Evangelicals. Senator Joe Lieberman came as "an observant Jew" to praise the Evangelicals' belated discovery of "the environment" in their new political platform, while Senator Sam Brownback of Kansas lauded them for taking a firm stand against prison rape.

"This is a young movement," Senator Brownback told Laurie Goodstein of the *New York Times*, "and it's just starting to get its sea legs. I think you'll now see it spread out into a whole lot of areas."

The plans for spreading out into a whole lot of areas was in fact what the NAE was trumpeting to the press at this conference, issuing a document called *For the Health of the Nation: An Evangelical Call to Civic Responsibility.*

Feeling their muscle after the 2004 presidential campaign, the Evangelicals were aiming now to spread their net beyond the two issues that compose the real heart, motivation, activism, spirit, and aim of their movement today: ending abortion under any circumstances, and ending the rights of gays and lesbians not only to be married but even to be protected by law against discrimination. This double-barreled blast has almost become—or replaced—their theology. If typical Evangelicals were asked on a lie-detector test to state their basic beliefs, it would probably be some version of pro-life and antigay before they even got to Jesus or Christianity, much less the Sermon on the Mount, which many in their ranks now believe was not intended for the times we live in (which handily relieves them of any regard for, among other blessings, peace and mercy). The preamble to the *Call to Civic Responsibility* states:

Evangelical Christians in America face a historic opportunity. We make up fully one quarter of all voters in the most powerful nation in history. Never before has God given American evangelicals such an awesome opportunity to shape public policy in ways that could contribute to the well-being of the entire world. Disengagement is not an option. We must seek God's face for biblical faithfulness and abundant wisdom to rise to this unique challenge.

This new declaration "for the health of the nation" not only implies a kind of grand entitlement—as if the Evangelicals finally have decided to come to our aid—but gives pause to non-Evangelicals with the uneasy thought that our own personal health care may in fact be influenced by the Evangelical vote in elections to come. If you're counting on some support for government aid from these antigovernment missionaries, forget about it.

Yet the new Evangelical platform of "civic responsibility" sounded as if it were written by a liberal Rip e-Van-gelical Winkle who went to sleep in the nineteenth century and has just awoken in the new millennium. This Evangelical Winkle must have looked around, blinked his long-closed eyes, and seen for the first time the issues that needed to be addressed:

racial injustice, poverty, human rights, religious freedom, and environmentalism. The most shocking—and puzzling— proposal from these superpatriot backers of the Bush war in Iraq was the stated goal of pursuing "thoroughly nonviolent paths to peace before resorting to military force" and the proviso that "if governments are going to use military force, they must use it in the service of peace and not merely in their national interest."

There was no mention, however, of plans for the first Evangelical antiwar rally.

These radical new public policies for Evangelicals were made acceptable to both the conservative and the liberal wings of their movement, according to the authors of the document, by setting "goals" for the issues but not the actual methods to carry them out. It was clear that even the abstract "goals" troubled some of the leaders at the conference. Some worried that the real goals of the movement might be lost or given less attention by all these new issues. Tom Minnery, vice president of Focus on the Family, headquartered in Colorado Springs (earthly heaven and haven of the Religious Right), wanted to get back to basics. "The issues of marriage, the issues of pro-life, are the issues that define us to this day," he pointed out, reminding the troops that their bread and butter was based on being antigay and antiabortion, never mind this talk about poverty and human rights.

Mr. Minnery also articulated the more conventional attitude of Evangelicals about environmentalism. At the luncheon, Senator Lieberman had praised the plank for caring about the environment and urged Evangelical support for a bill he was cosponsoring with Senator John McCain to work against global

warming by putting a curb on heat-trapping gases. No doubt
seeing this as a devil-inspired distraction from their mission
against gay rights and abortion, Mr. Minnery stood up and
warned his fellow Evangelicals against getting off the track:
"Do not make this about global warming!"

Minnery need not fear that the environmental aspect of the
NAE's new *Call to Civic Responsibility* will transform Evangelicals into Greenpeaceniks. Shunning even the *word* "environmentalism," which the Religious Right has traditionally
opposed for interfering with "free market values" (i.e., profi-
teering from stripping the land of its remaining natural
resources), the brave new NAE effort is called "stewardship of
creation" or "creation care."

None of the afternoon NAE speakers addressed this delicate
subject, which had already alarmed Religious Right political
heroes like Senator James Inhofe of Oklahoma, who called up
NAE president Ted Haggard to warn him that it sounded like
left-wing radicals were trying to bamboozle unsuspecting
Evangelicals into their cause; on his Web site, Inhofe calls envi-
ronmentalist groups "snake-oil salesmen out to mislead the
public." Pat Robertson was so concerned about the threat that
he featured Senator Inhofe on his TV show—whom he
described as "a strong critic of the excesses of the environmen-
talist movement."

Pat Robertson got to the heart of the matter when he asked
Senator Inhofe if "environmental concerns" were "sort of like a
God" to the radical left. Citing Romans 1:22, and 23, the bibli-
cally well-versed senator affirmed Robertson's fear:

You quit worshipping God and start worshipping the creation—
the creeping things, the four-legged beasts, the birds and all that.
If you read Romans 1:25, it says "and they gave up their God and
started worshipping the creation." That's what we are looking at
now, that's what's going on. And we can't let it happen.

In an interview in the *New York Times* a few weeks after
the NAE conference, Richard Cizik, the NAE vice president
for governmental affairs, attempted to soothe such fears
when he made clear that the Evangelicals were not adopting
the cause of "environmentalism" but, rather, of *creation
care.*" The *Times'* Deborah Solomon said it sounded like "a
division of Medicare" and wondered what was wrong with
the term "environmentalism." Rev. Cizik explained that the
word "environmentalism" had "a bad reputation among
Evangelicals" because its advocates relied on big-government
solutions, allied themselves with population-control groups,
and, perhaps most damning of all, "they keep kooky religious
company." He charged that some environmentalists are
"pantheists who believe creation itself is holy, not the Creator." To assure the faithful that the NAE wasn't joining
forces with a bunch of Godless pantheists, Rev. Cizik reported
that he had met with representatives of the Sierra Club and
the National Wildlife Federation and told them he didn't
plan on any "formal collaboration." Hopefully now Tom Minnery, Pat Robertson, and Senator Inhofe can sleep soundly
again.

The difficulties of reconciling the new "call to responsibility"
laid out when the liberal Rip e-Van-gelical Winkle woke up

and saw what was going on in the world were apparent in the contradictions and challenges that emerged in the rest of the conference session. Diane Knippers, president of the influential Institute for Religion and Democracy (IRD), spoke about the growing power of Evangelicals within the mainline denominations, citing their influence in the Methodist, Presbyterian, and Episcopal churches.

Mrs. Knippers, one of the most popular leaders of the Religious Right, died of cancer at age fifty-three a month after the conference, prompting a mainline liberal church leader to observe with respect that "Her passing was a big loss for the Religious Right and especially the IRD—she put a good face on what they were doing."

Mrs. Knippers' pleasant image as the housewife next-door belied her tough political activism in the religious wars, where she was a leader in the Episcopal opposition to the appointment of an openly gay bishop in New Hampshire and a continually outspoken opponent of the mainline National Council of Churches and World Council of Churches, accusing them of leftist politics and urging member churches to withdraw funding from both bodies. As president of the IRD, she was a key leader in the movement to turn mainline churches from liberal religion to Evangelical principles and enlist their members in the battle against gay rights and abortion.

Mrs. Knippers' IRD accuses the mainline churches of throwing themselves into "leftist crusades"—including some of the policies adopted in the Evangelicals' *Call to Civic Responsibility* that she endorsed, including "environmentalism, pacifism, and multiculturalism." She made no attempt to explain such seeming contradictions in the policies of her organizations. In her talk she accused not only mainline leaders but also "the Evangelical left" (the first hint of the day that such a thing existed) of exerting "pacifist influences in academic circles." She did not attempt to explain how that criticism jibed with the peace language of *The Call to Civic Responsibility*, which states, "We urge followers of Jesus to engage in practical peacemaking locally, nationally, and internationally."

It will take a while for Evangelical leaders to justify their new "civic responsibility" with the basic attitudes and practices they are known for. Mrs. Knippers acknowledged that "the jewel in the crown of mainline social activism was the civil rights movement"—a movement most Evangelicals suspected was communist-inspired and stayed clear of, but now they are apologizing to African-American believers and trying to recruit them for their own forces, providing greater numbers in the battle to theologize America. In the new *Call*, Rip e-Van-gelical has discovered that "America has a tragic history of mistreating Native Americans, the cruel practice of slavery, and the subsequent segregation and exploitation of the descendants of slaves." (Remember, you heard it here last.)

Mrs. Knippers was at her best in going back to chew on the more familiar meat of Evangelical rhetoric as she explained how the mainline churches had, with the rest of the culture, turned left in the sixties and lost their soul.

After "the jewel" of their civil rights action, mainline churches, Mrs. Knippers said, fell into "less beneficial causes," and she enumerated them:

The anti–Vietnam War movement produced an antipathy to much of what the United States represented, leading to naïve support for Marxist-Leninist causes until the fall of the Berlin Wall. Women's liberation developed into radical, neopagan feminism. Today that movement, more than anything else, represents the celebration of lesbianism and the endorsement of the entire gay, lesbian, bisexual, transgendered agenda.

It was now time for Rip e-Van-gelical to face his sins of the past—in this case, his big sleep during the civil rights movement. Having now discovered that "racism still makes many African Americans, Hispanics, and other ethnic minorities particularly vulnerable to a variety of social ills," the Evangelicals have luckily been able to dig up a biblical passage that justified human equality. In their new "call" to responsibility they cited Romans 10:12: "For there is no difference between the Jew and the Greek: for the same Lord over all is rich unto all that call upon him." If that does it for them, it's a shame that their theologians, who inspect the Bible like Sherlock Holmes looking for clues with his giant magnifying glass to justify all their pet prejudices, skipped over this one while their mainline brethren were risking their lives on Freedom Rides and voter registration drives.

As penance for their historic oversight, the NAE had invited an African-American minister to tell them in person why it was that he and his fellow black Christians who shared many theological beliefs with the Evangelicals found it difficult to identify with them. Dr. James Love, pastor of Faith Tabernacle United Holy Church in Washington, D.C., is an articulate, forty-something preacher who speaks with a natural eloquence and a nice sense of irony and wit. His talk to the NAE was titled "Why are African-American Christians reticent in identifying themselves as Evangelicals?"

Rev. Love began by telling how he had "struggled with the label 'Evangelical'" since his undergraduate days at Lincoln University, a historical black college. "To me, Evangelicals are identified with people like Jerry Falwell and institutions like Bob Jones University," Rev. Love explained:

> They had no interest in civil rights, the black struggle for freedom and justice. They were religiously conservative, even narrow-minded; socially, they were harbingers of the status quo, without compunction for inequities that blacks suffered in racist society. I guess what was extremely problematical for me was the conspicuous absence of white Evangelicals in the civil rights movement for black enfranchisement and justice. Why didn't they support the Montgomery bus boycott? Where were they in Birmingham? The sad fact is, that it was mainline liberals who stood shoulder to shoulder with King, Abernathy, and Young. Didn't the white Evangelicals know that righteousness and justice are fundamental to the character of God?

For biblical backing, Rev. Love cited Psalms 89:14: "Justice and judgment are the habitation of thy throne: mercy and truth shall go before thy face." Too bad the Evangelical scholars missed that one as they pored over every verse in the Bible, building entire theologies out of parsing sentences and finding the word "rapture" in a code only they have to the Book of Revelations.

Rev. Love said that over the years he had talked with many African-American religious leaders, asking why they were reticent to call themselves Evangelicals when they held many of the same views about their faith and the Bible. He had summarized the answers in five points that laid it on the line:

1. Evangelism is somehow identified with whiteness. White Evangelicals assumed the role of spokespeople for God in America. Thus, from an African-American perspective evangelicism is seen as "the white man's religion."
2. Psychologically, African Americans perceive that white Evangelicals have underappreciated, have undervalued, and have marginalized their religious experience and their leadership.
3. African Americans who desired theological training were not permitted to enroll in conservative white Bible schools or seminaries. Dr. Tony Evans, in his book *Let's Get to Know Each Other*, stated that "Dallas Theological Seminary did not admit Blacks until 1968!"
4. White Evangelicals did not stand with African Americans during the civil rights struggle for justice and freedom in the 1950s and 1960s. Yet, in spite of this, Reverend Samuel Hines, the late pastor of Third Street Church of God in Washington, D.C., said, "We need each other because of the interdependence of community; we all hold the key to other people's freedom. White people can't free themselves of the oppression and injustices . . . Racial divisions are robbing both sides." I quote from *Christianity Today*, the 1993 article "We Need Each Other."
5. African-Americans tend to see the connection between individual sin and its effect upon social institutions. Therefore, we view social justice as part of the gospel ministry.

Adding to his enlightening message to the white NAE, Rev. Love said, "I agree with Dr. Tony Evans when he said 'The

black Church was evangelical long before Harold John Ock-
enga [a white theologian] coined the term 'Evangelical.'"

Rev. Love concluded that African Americans are still leery
about identifying as Evangelical "because of the social and
political connotations of the term," but, he said, the term
"doesn't have to have a political connotation; it can and must
return to its basic definition: the Good News of Jesus Christ."

That's an ideal vision, but it is impossible now for the Evangelicals to shake off the image they have made for themselves
up until now as ultraconservative Republicans who are rigid on
their key issues because they have convinced themselves—if not
the rest of the world—that God is on their side.

They are, however, trying to reach out to African-American
Evangelicals like Dr. Love and, based on their common theological outlook, trying to bring these formerly alienated sheep
back into the fold. The African-American Evangelicals were
never "lost" to their religion—they were in fact the most vital
practitioners of it—but the white shepherds had treated them
like the "black sheep" of their movement, ignoring their needs
and causes and, like other segregationists, refusing to recognize
their very humanity (as they now refuse to recognize the
humanity of gays and lesbians). As the politically left Evangelical Jim Wallis has remarked, "You wonder what happened to
George Wallace and his racist followers? They put on perfume
and called themselves 'the Religious Right.'"

A reporter in the audience asked Rev. Love whether, despite
the past neglect and abuse of the white Evangelical establishment
toward African Americans, there was any hope of reconciliation.

Rev. Love nodded and said:

The black and white liberal establishment is no longer the only player for the consciousness of black and white people. A lot of us are saying to old guard liberals "We thought that way for forty years and it isn't getting that much better." Poverty among blacks, number of blacks in jail, has increased. So some of us in the New Guard are thinking that we aren't necessarily Democratic and were not necessarily Republican. We're Independent. Our attitude is "Show me what you got, and I'll look at it and make up my mind."

Another questioner asked Dr. Wenz if the NAE was making any progress in getting African Americans back into their ranks. "As more Asians, Hispanics, and other ethnic groups have come to our Evangelical churches," Dr. Wenz answered, "we are breaking down old barriers, and we hope that process continues with our African-American brothers."

Rev. Love affirmed that:

There's a groundswell of conservative black preachers—like Bishop Harry Long in Atlanta, who has one of the largest churches in the country—and he and others are moving in a direction of traditional values and away from the old-boy, old-guard mind-set. We want to be more self-sufficient, self-supporting, and we don't see the government as the panacea to cure all of our ills.

There was hopeful applause from the Evangelicals present, and an outbreak of laptop-tapping among reporters.

This potential alliance of black and white Evangelicals has not only historic religious import but even greater political consequences. George Bush got a higher percentage of African-American votes than any previous Republican candidate, though it still remained small. If the white Evangelical establishment is able to bring more blacks into its camp, they will also be bringing more votes to the GOP that were once counted safe for the Democrats.

One of the Evangelicals wondered why Dr. Wenz didn't get together to talk about these issues with Rev. Love every week as a process of reuniting their races and their religion. Dr. Wenz explained that as much as he'd like to do that, he lives in Colorado Springs now, and Rev. Love's church is in Washington, D.C., so it wouldn't be very easy, though they were friends and would certainly keep in touch. It evidently did not occur to the Evangelical questioner that perhaps he might find his own African-American friend to talk with.

Rev. Love and Dr. Wenz engaged in a comradely hug of Evangelical fellowship, which brought more applause and an upbeat conclusion to the program.

† † †

The next morning I went to the Ramada Inn in suburban Virginia to interview Dr. Wenz over coffee in the crowded dining room. He had just been served a stack of pancakes, and I said I'd be glad to wait until he was finished with breakfast, but he graciously waved me to the chair across the table from him and said we could begin. I turned on my tape recorder and asked when the Evangelicals' new outreach to their African-American brethren had started.

"We're just now waking up," he said. "My generation needs to be the catalyst, and my children's generation needs to bring it to fulfillment."

Why did it take so long, I wondered, and why did white Evangelicals "sit out" the civil rights movement instead of "sitting in" like the mainline Christians who supported Dr. King? After all the same Bible verses the Evangelicals use to support their commitment to minorities now were already in the Bible in the fifties.

"We can only write it off to fear, primarily of change," Dr. Wenz said:

> There was and often is in the Church—not just Evangelical—a desire to keep the status quo. There's no use affixing blame at this point—we missed it. It's myopic—a matter of having blinders on. It doesn't mean every Evangelical said, "Lets see what we can do to stifle the civil rights movement." Look back at the agencies who feared Martin Luther King was a communist. Fear of communism was great, and there were lots of other fears swirling in the air. What do you do when you're afraid—you hunker down. It really was a kind of hunker-down mentality.

I asked Dr. Wenz how his own interest in the African-American community and his friendship with Rev. Love had come about. He answered:

I'd been pastor of a predominantly Anglo congregation in Maryland and I was asked to come to the city [Washington, D.C.] to teach in a school operated by the Christian Missionary Alliance, where the faculty and students were predominantly Afro-American. The dean is a friend of mine, and he called and said "We need somebody to teach here." I taught one or two courses a semester at the D.C. campus of Nyack College in addition to my pastoral ministry. The main campus is in Nyack, New York, and it is one of the most ethnically diverse colleges in the country.

It's been a wonderful experience for me. I had students who said "Professor, I can't make it in today because I don't have enough money to get on the Metro." All of a sudden you realize you're not dealing with college students who are away at school living in the dorm and having a good time. Most of them are working full-time and going to school—I learned so much in the process of teaching and loving my students, and I think it was reciprocated. Jim Love, the African-American pastor you heard speak yesterday, is a dear friend, and our talks together have been very important to me.

The day before, Dr. Wenz had said the number of Evangelicals in Congress is roughly equal to or a little higher than the number of Evangelicals in the general population, and they are on the Hill representing their constituents with a Christian worldview. A speaker at the luncheon had charged that the Evangelicals use the issues of abortion and gay rights as a "litmus test" for Christians, when the only "litmus test" should be the Gospels, the first four books of the New Testament—Matthew, Mark, Luke, and John—which tell the story of Jesus.

I asked Dr. Wenz whether he thought the millions of Christians like myself who belong to mainline Protestant churches "shared a Christian worldview" if we were pro-choice and upheld gay rights. On the issue of gays, he said:

As Evangelicals we don't want to have a "This is wrong don't do it" attitude without recognizing the complexity of the issue. We don't have a clear answer for why people are homosexual . . . Our reason for opposing the gay lifestyle is based on our Christian view that says God created marriage and did so because it promotes our health and well-being. Deviations from that lifestyle— one man, one woman for a lifetime—bring on disease and suicide, and psychological problems just escalate. I'm not talking just about homosexuals, I'm talking about people who are openly promiscuous. God gave us marriage because it is good and promotes health. Radical feminists who say marriage is an oppressive institution, mistakenly believe that because some people have had an oppressive marriage the institution is fatally flawed—but its humanity that's fatally flawed.

On the issue of pro-choice, Dr. Wenz said:

Women in most cases do have a choice—abstinence is a choice, contraception is a choice. The Catholic Church would disagree with us. We object to abortion simply as a means of contraception. The reason for that is a deep-seated belief from Scripture that God is the author of life—He gives life—and that which is in fact human life should be regarded as a treasure given from God. Whether that is a two-celled embryo—a zygote—or whether that is a five-and-a-half-month-old fetus, to treat it as simply a commodity is a dangerous and tragic thing.

We live in a conflicted culture where in the same hospital with two rooms right next to each other, Mrs. Johnson is having a baby that's four months premature, and they will spend a hundred thousand dollars for that baby who's a preemie, a hundred feet down the hall they're aborting a woman at eight months. Someone has got to sort that out for me. We have not as a culture satisfactorily answered the question "What is human life, what does it come from, and why is it special?"

This is a complex issue. Some Evangelicals don't nuance this—if you're going to be antiabortion, you better run some clinics to give women some options. It's not enough to say "This is wrong; you can't do it."

Dr. Wenz' explanation of the Evangelical "litmus tests" was indeed more "nuanced" than most of the hard-line Religious Right rhetoric on the subject, but it still left out millions of mainline churchgoers whose "Christian worldview" is pro-choice and pro–gay rights.

"I understand that," he said:

I understand the position that Hillary Clinton is trying to stake out—that in order to appeal to or at least to accommodate Evangelicals and conservatives, in terms of "I want to preserve abortion but I want it to be rare—safe and rare." What's made this difficult is that on some issues conservatives and liberals—not just Evangelicals—have polarized—and for some of them, there is no middle ground. What we get is increasingly heated rhetoric

on both sides. That's the liberals who say if you require a fifteen-
year-old girl to get permission from her parents to have an abortion, we're in trouble.

I asked Dr. Wenz if that meant he felt Hillary's position is
valid, that it's still within a "Christian worldview"?
Wenz winced, and shook his head:

I'm not going to say that—lest everybody would quote me. I will
say that what she's attempting to do is carve out a middle position. The question is will everybody meet her in the middle? I
don't know.

While we care about the preservation of marriage and we care
about abortion, those are not the only social issues we need to
address. There's a sense in which, as Evangelicals, we're recognizing that we need to open up our vision to a wider panorama.
This is a challenging endeavor because it's calling Evangelicals to
a broader understanding of the social responsibilities of the
Gospel than we had in the fifties.

The "wider panorama" that NAE leaders like Dr. Wenz are
becoming active in means increasing recruitment of Evangelical troops. The mainline churches for the most part seem
unaware of such new possibilities. Nearly all of them stick to
the same routines of the past, throwing in some TV advertising
as if it's magic, and brood over declining membership.

"I pastored a church in Rockville, Maryland, for twelve
years," Dr. Wenz said:

and in that period, the population of Montgomery County, Maryland, went from being twenty-four percent foreign born to forty-eight percent foreign born. Nearly half the people who live in the county now were not born in the U.S. My congregation launched an international ministry to that community primarily as a vehicle for teaching English as a Second Language. We ran an ESL [English as a Second Language] program, and on any given night we'd have ninety to a hundred students from twenty-five different countries. And we taught them English.

I doubt that was all they taught them. It's a good bet their new vocabulary includes words that are linked together, such as "evil" and "abortion," "gay" and "sin," and on a more worldly note, "Republican" and "Christian." It's a real bargain for the immigrants—they learn to speak English and become Evangelicals at the same time. I know of no mainline churches that carry out such a program.

While the new Evangelical *Call* is still mostly rhetoric and in many ways misleading, it can still be pointed to as NAE "policy." In that way it co-opts the territory that the mainline denominations and the liberal Catholics could once claim as their own. While the *Call* embodies the sincere social action beliefs of some Evangelicals who are pushing for change, it papers over the still hardy racism and other deep-seated prejudices of the movement that Robert Wenz frankly admits will take a generation or so to heal.

The irony of their proud *Evangelical Call to Civic Responsibility* is that some of their fellow Evangelicals have been calling out to them for decades to recognize these issues. Jim Wallis has been working to relieve poverty throughout his career and formed his Call to Renewal movement in 1995 to include more groups in joining the cause. Wallis and his magazine *Sojourners*, have long been considered too far left to be counted as one of the NAE's own, though he says he's been welcomed by some of them since the success of his bestseller. Dr. Wenz is not among them. When I asked him about Wallis, he said, "I haven't read his book. I stopped reading *Sojourners* because there's too much guilt. In the long term, guilt causes avoidance. We're not going to motivate anyone with guilt."

I said that I get the feeling Wallis is thought of as a "fringe" person in the NAE. Dr. Wenz nodded, saying "Mmm-hmmm." I pointed out that the NAE is now stating the kind of beliefs Wallis has advocated for several decades in its new *Call to Civic Responsibility*. Does this mean he will become a more significant voice in the NAE?

"I'm not sure I can answer that," Dr. Wenz said. "Maybe Rich Cizik can give you a better 'read' on that than I can."

I e-mail Rev. Cizik that I'd like to interview him, but he doesn't respond.

† † †

Had members of the NAE felt a little guilt about the issues they had neglected for so long, it might not have taken them more than a quarter-century to acknowledge and make use of the work of one of their own most articulate voices against the evil of poverty, Ronald J. Sider. I was told that Ron Sider, a theologian and professor emeritus at Eastern University, was the person most responsible for composing the Evangelicals' long-belated *Call to Civic Responsibility*. His book *Rich Christians in an Age of Hunger* was a bestseller when it was published in 1977 and is still in print in new editions, yet its powerful message, not only on poverty but also on "environmental decay," is only now being incorporated into the language—if not the actions—of the NAE.

Long before Jim Wallis's bestseller appeared on the scene to remind us of all the references to poverty in the Bible, Professor Sider wrote that "Hundreds of Biblical texts tell us that God still measures our societies by what we do to the poorest," and he reminds us in his latest edition that 34,000 children die of starvation and preventable diseases every day.

In 2005, Ron Sider scorched the NAE with his latest book *The Scandal of the Evangelical Conscience*, in which he revealed that polls by Gallup and the Barna Group showed that "Divorce is more common among 'born-again' Christians than in the general American population . . . White Evangelicals are the *most* likely people to object to neighbors of another race."

It took the NAE some thirty years to adopt some of the rhetoric, if not the action, of Ron Sider's call to Christians for responsibility on poverty; only their God knows how long it will take them to acknowledge his exposé of the "family values" they so piously boast about. I wonder if James Dobson, the hard-line Religious Right head of Focus on the Family has read in Ron Sider's *Scandal* that:

One important study found that "less than 3 percent of wives in egalitarian marriages had been beaten by their husbands in the previous year." In traditional marriages where the husband was dominant, 10.7 percent of wives had been beaten—a rate of violence more than 300 percent higher than for egalitarian marriage.

"It is doubtless painful for the ladies to hear," Pat Robertson said, "but if you get married, you have accepted the headship of a man, your husband. Christ is the head of the household and the husband is the head of the wife, and that's the way it is, period."

With all its boasting of new political power as well as its misleading image of moral superiority, the NAE, in the time of its newfound fame and glory, is trying to straddle two disparate positions—the hard-line, Religious Right followers of Robertson and Falwell and the younger, more progressive activists and mavericks. Middle-of-the-road leaders like NAE veep Robert Wenz are embarrassed by the televangelists but unable to disown them for fear of losing their base.

Trying to ride two horses at the same time will be no easy task for the NAE—as Republicans and Democrats alike can testify. As Robert Wenz reminded the conference in D.C., NAE president Ted Haggard "was elected by a body of thirty million people, and we would encourage you to talk with him if you really want to find out what Evangelicals are thinking."

I found out. So did everyone else who follows the news after Pat Robertson on his national TV show said the United States should kill Hugo Chavez, the leftist Venezuelan president who expressed his fear of the United States. "If he thinks we're going to assassinate him, we should go ahead and do it," Robertson told the audience of his TV program *The 700 Club*.

Assassinating Venezuela's president, Robertson explained, is "a whole lot cheaper than starting a war."

Most progressive Christians, including those who are Evangelicals, as well as Jews, Muslims, Buddhists, agnostics, atheists —and, I would guess, the leaders of the NBA, NFL, and major league baseball—either condemned or ridiculed Robertson's proposal, or both. Many conservative Christian groups, however, including the Traditional Values Coalition, the Family Research Council, and the Christian Coalition, told Laurie Goodstein of the *New York Times* that they "were too busy to comment" on Robertson's assassination proposal.

When asked his opinion, NAE president Ted Haggard explained that Robertson's program is divided into two parts— one part of the show is "religious," while in the other part Robertson is speaking as "a pundit." It was in his role as "a pundit," Haggard explained, that he advocated the assassination of the Venezuelan president. Evidently, the president of the National Association of Evangelicals believed that either made it all right or at least absolved "religion."

I think I can guess which way the NAE is heading—as well as who in their ranks is going with them—and, more important, who is not. Those who are in the process of breaking ranks are going to make a significant impact on the religious-political alignments of this country.

III.

How They Hijacked Jesus

A woman with her gray hair coiled around the back of her head sat behind a battered old desk listening intently to the babble of a shabbily dressed drunk woman. As people wandered in and out of the room, a young medical student from Columbia University shifted from one foot to the other, impatiently waiting to speak to the sober and serious-looking woman. Finally the sober woman who sat behind the desk took her attention from the drunken woman across from her, looked up at the medical student, smiled, and asked, "Did you wish to speak with one of us?"

Young Robert Coles, the future psychiatrist, author, and

Harvard professor, wrote that in that moment he "got" who Dorothy Day was. He later wrote a book about her and her work at the Catholic Worker "Hospitality House" that she ran in the Bowery in New York City and the newspaper of the same name that she wrote for and edited, a newspaper that sold all over the country for a penny a copy. Michael Harrington was inspired by what he learned while living at the Catholic Worker to write *The Other America*, a book that became the inspiration of Lyndon Johnson's poverty program.

A militant postcollegiate atheist of the time, I was moved to write about Dorothy Day in an early article in *The Nation* and later went to the day care center some of her followers started on East 100th Street in New York, where I soon moved to live and write a book about the neighborhood, *Island in the City*. Many intellectuals in New York in the fifties were moved and impressed by Dorothy Day and her Catholic Workers as well as the men and women of the storefront churches known as the East Harlem Protestant Parish, because they practiced rather than preached their Christian faith.

Those were inspiring exceptions to the "country club Christianity" that was booming in the plush years after World War II, with churches vying to build higher spires than their rivals and offering religion as a key to success in business. Norman Vincent Peale was preaching the popular gospel of positive thinking at Marble Collegiate Church in Manhattan, Jesus was painted with a smile on his face (presumably not a crucifixion likeness), and a Methodist magazine called *Together* selected an "All-Methodist Football Team." (Charles Keysor, a *Together* editor, bobbed up again in the seventies as an influential early player in the Religious Right.) In the fifties, God was in his American heaven, making sure we didn't fall prey to "Godless communism" (though to be on the safe side, we built even bigger and deadlier atomic bombs and home fallout shelters to hide from the communists' bombs), and all seemed right with the Church. Roman Catholics, who were still looked on with nervous suspicion by many American Protestants (in 1960 John F. Kennedy had to reassure voters that if elected he would not follow orders from the pope), were made to seem less threatening by Bishop Fulton J. Sheen, whose prime-time half-hour TV show topped the Nielsen ratings. The appeal of Bishop Sheen to Middle America was brought home to me when I came back to Indianapolis on vacation from college in New York in the fifties to find that my Kentucky-bred Baptist father and Missouri-Presbyterian mother ordered all guests and relatives—including their atheist-pinko son—to gather before the TV when Bishop Sheen, in full Roman Catholic regalia, held forth with his weekly homily.

Fundamentalists and their Evangelical kin were safely sequestered in the hills and hollows of the Southern countryside, preaching that quaint old-time religion of hellfire and damnation while still licking their wounds from the Scopes trial. Benign Evangelist Billy Graham inspired and comforted many and threatened no one except the Devil he preached against, his preaching inspiring thousands to walk down the same sawdust trail blazed by Billy Sunday at revivals in stadiums around the country in the 1910s. Mainline Christianity in America after World War II, like the Maginot Line in France before the war, was thought to be impregnable.

Spencer Rice, who preaches now at "the church of the presidents" in Washington, D.C., was ordained as an Episcopal minister in 1955 and recalls:

> After World War II there was a burst of religious enthusiasm—it seemed like there was a church building on every corner. The mainline churches were so enthusiastic about being successful, there were no deep religious roots. There was an idea that Christianity was just a matter of building churches and expanding, without looking at the world around us and the problems around us.
>
> In 1958 I attended a conference in Santa Barbara at which twenty-five prominent rectors came to look at the future of the Episcopal Church, and we were guided by three sociologists from UCLA who were not church members, and so carried no baggage of preconceptions. They said the Pentecostal, Evangelical churches in the U.S. are going to grow at an exponential rate, and the mainline churches are going to recede dramatically. That was shocking, but I passed it on at a deanery meeting, and a retired bishop said, "Well, now, that can't happen."

If the Christian mainline establishment in this country anticipated any kind of trouble, competition, or infiltration, it was surely from the Godless communists of the Soviet Union or the sneaky Reds in government. Surely no threat to their dominance could come from "that ol' time religion" of Evangelicals and Fundamentalists that up in the Eastern Establishment was thought to be of interest only to mandolin-pickin' hillbillies or hallelujah-shoutin' "colored folks," the polite term for the people known then as Negroes (pronounced *knee-grows*).

Joseph Hough Jr., looking back now from his view in the president's office of Union Theological Seminary, remembers otherwise:

> I grew up in the South, and if you lived down there you could see the Evangelical and Fundamentalist strength all along. After the Scopes trial, Fundamentalism was wounded, and it decided it was going to be a religion of true believers in an alien culture. They had been ridiculed, humiliated, and people said, "Well, so much for that movement." My grandfather thought evolution was an invention of the Devil. Nobody was going to tell *him* he was descended from a monkey.

Dr. Hough shakes his head, smiles, and looks at me over the top of his glasses to comment: "I take the argument the other way—I have too much respect for monkeys."

"But fundamentalism became a private thing," he goes on, "a transaction with God so you could go to Heaven and not Hell, and the way to do that was to not believe all this tomfoolery you heard coming from college professors and intellectuals—so they went underground. They weren't organized, but they were there."

If there was any last gasp of social or religious influence on the country at large from that sector of the population, it was surely drowned out by the coming of the Beatles. John Lennon proclaimed that the Beatles were "bigger than Christ," and millions of teenagers around the world seemed to support the notion in the 1960s. There was little doubt that Paul, George, Ringo, and John were more well-known worldwide—and surely more adored by the younger generation of the era—than Matthew, Mark, Luke, and John.

The other voice that stirred the country and awakened the mainline churches out of their dozing self-satisfaction was that of a charismatic young Negro minister in Alabama who based his social revolution and use of nonviolent tactics on the life and teachings of Jesus. The message and the courage of Martin Luther King Jr. inspired white ministers and parishioners to leave their Northern comfort and march by his side, along with idealistic young men and women from all across the country who put their lives on the line and in some cases lost them in a cause larger than themselves.

Around the time of the crushing Republican presidential defeat of 1964, the liberal mainline churches were enjoying their finest hours, as many of their leaders and laypeople joined forces with Martin Luther King in what became the victorious battles of the civil rights movement. It looked as if the liberals had surely established their dominance in American Protestantism and could look forward to more and greater victories for the principles set out by Jesus in the Sermon on the Mount: victories for peace, for the poor, for the meek, the mourners, the pure in heart, the persecuted.

"Civil rights was the peak of the influence of liberal religion on public policy, and I think it capped," Joseph Hough Jr. could see, looking back from 2005. "A little after that, civil rights wasn't just a religious movement, it was also a popular movement based on equal rights. It was hard to be openly opposed to civil rights. Religion framed itself as the inheritor of civil rights guarantees."

What Henry James called "the figure in the carpet" is the design underneath, the one we can't see from the outside, from the surface pattern of the times we are living in. How could any citizen doubt that equality and the forces that brought it about were here to stay when the Texan president Lyndon Johnson stood before Congress and the people of the United States and recited the mantra Martin Luther King had made sacred to the secular as well as the religious: *"We shall overcome."*

The awakening and response to the civil rights movement was indeed, as Diane Knippers put it, "the jewel in the crown of mainline social activism," but it was not untarnished—like most genuine jewels, it cost a great deal for the clergy who were cast out by their own flocks.

In some cases ministers lost their pulpits and their livelihoods, for by no means did all Christians, either North or South, want to hear—much less respond to—the words of Jesus when they were put into action in their own time and their own country rather than safely frozen in hymnals and prayer books used only for an hour on Sunday mornings and stowed away until the following week.

† † †

Across the street from Joe Hough's office at Union Theological Seminary stands a massive, imposing building that wears no crosses or religious symbols on its outer walls but is known to its occupants and neighbors as "The God Box." The Interfaith Building houses many of the national headquarters of the mainline Protestant denominations, one of which is the United

Methodist Church, whose Women's Division is headed by Jan Love, an articulate, attractive blonde woman who formerly taught politics and religion at the University of South Carolina and served on the central committee of the World Council of Churches.

Ms. Love is self-described as "a preacher's kid" who grew up in Alabama and remembers that:

> Pastors in the sixties were run off by congregations all over the place. My pastor father was run out of churches—it was hard as hell. When I was five years old we were attacked by the Ku Klux Klan—my first clear indication that religion and politics were intimately connected.
>
> My father tried to support a bus boycott in Mobile like the one in Montgomery with some other white and African-American pastors. The white pastor who led the effort had to go to New York City. Every one or two years we had to move—one time the Klan burned a cross at our house. They served as alternative police, and some *were* police. The cross they burned in front of our house was constructed in the parking lot of the police station. The church cut off my father's salary. We had to keep moving— and it doesn't take long to exhaust the rural towns in Alabama.

Rev. William Sloane Coffin, then chaplain of Yale, was the first of the Northern white ministers to go South in the cause of civil rights. He joined Martin Luther King's troops on one of the first Freedom Rides and spent a night in jail in Alabama, making a headline in the *New York Times*: "Yale's Chaplain among 11 Seized in Montgomery." With a natural gift for turning the right phrase for the media, Coffin became a national leader and spokesperson for the civil rights movement and for liberal mainline churches.

Spencer Rice thinks the clergy was ready for a challenge that applied their Christianity to injustices in their own world: "In the sixties there was a reaction against the idea that Christianity and religion [were] just a matter of building churches and expanding."

But many conservative churchgoers were disturbed when their own ministers joined the battle and took the teachings of Jesus off the pulpit and into the world. In applying the Christian message to the racial crisis in America, these ministers followed the leadership of their fellow Christian pastor, Reverend King. Many church members looked upon this with shock, as if in practicing what they preached, their pastors had committed a breach of faith—or at least of etiquette.

That kind of division was primarily a Northern issue, since except for the black churches and leaders in the South who supported Dr. King, the white Protestant clergy below the Mason-Dixon Line believed with the great majority of their flocks that "civil rights" were really "civil wrongs," as Rev. Jerry Falwell declared from the pulpit of his prospering Thomas Road Baptist Church in Lynchburg, Virginia. Rev. Falwell was hardly alone or original in attacking Dr. King and his fellow civil rights leaders as leftist dupes and tools of the communists (after all, J. Edgar Hoover was disseminating the charges), but he may have been unique in coining a phrase that later took on an appropriate irony as he became a leader for the Religious/Political Right: "Preachers are not called to be politicians, but soul winners."

It was 1965, and the right-wing preachers had not yet discovered the benefits of delivering votes to the GOP along with souls to Jesus. Even above the Mason-Dixon Line, "Civil rights was controversial then, let's face it," I'm reminded by Diane Kessler, director of the Massachusetts Council of Churches. "Many clergy who became active and took the lead got burned often in their congregations, and the same happened with Vietnam."

Yet for many liberals, the antiwar movement during Vietnam was another "jewel in the crown" of Christian activism.

William Sloane Coffin carried on to protest the war, leading students in draft-card burnings and offering sanctuary to draft resisters in the chapel of Yale. Liberal mainline churchgoers were proud of their faith, as their kind of Christian Soldiers went to battle against segregation, discrimination, and war, opposing the national leaders and policies who supported those evils.

At the same time, protest against the war was a thorn—or more aptly, a metal spike—in the side of a number of mainline ministers whose congregations felt they'd become too radical, un-American, and, in the view of many conservative churchgoers, un-Christian.

Looking back, some mainline leaders today feel that the heavy emphasis on social action in the sixties came to replace theology in the religious life of their denominations. A case can be made that in fact social action "came to the rescue," for rather than replacing a theologically grounded faith, it was replacing a theologically sponsored "end of faith" that suddenly became a hot topic in the press as well as the seminaries. It was

Christian theologians, not secular critics, who declared in the sixties that "God is dead"—news that was regarded as important enough to make the cover of *Time*, and be reported in the major media.

† † †

God Is Dead in Georgia: Eminent Deity Succumbs during Surgery / Succession in Doubt as All Creation Groans
Special to the *New York Times:* Nov. 9 [1965]—God, creator of the universe, principal deity of the world's Jews, ultimate reality of Christians, and most eminent of all divinities, died late yesterday during major surgery undertaken to correct a massive diminishing influence.

His exact age is not known, but close friends estimate that it greatly exceeded that of all other extant beings. While he did not, in recent years, maintain any fixed abode, his house was said to consist of many mansions. . . .

[T]he deity's surgeon, Thomas J. J. Altizer, 38, of Emory University in Atlanta, indicated possible cardiac insufficiency. Assisting Dr. Altizer in the unsuccessful surgery were Dr. Paul van Buren of Temple University, Philadelphia and Dr. William Hamilton of Colgate-Rochester, N.Y.

Dr. Altizer, God's surgeon, in an exclusive interview with the *Times*, stated this morning that the death was "not unexpected. He had been ailing for some time," Dr. Altizer said, "and lived much longer than most of us thought possible." He noted that the death of God had, in fact, been prematurely announced in the last century by the famed German surgeon, Nietzsche. Nietzsche, who was insane the last ten years of his life, may have confused "certain symptoms of morbidity in the aged patient with actual death, a mistake any busy surgeon will occasionally make," Dr. Altizer suggested.

The above "news story" by Anthony Towne is only a satire but it was based on the earnest—and obviously influential— writings of the Christian theologians cited in the spoof: Thomas J. J. Altizer's "Christian atheism," William Hamilton's "religionless" approach, Paul van Buren's "secular gospel," and Gabriel Vahanian's analysis that God in the modern world "evaporates into a tragicomic, mythological atavism." The views of these scholars (who were based in leading universities and theological seminaries) were analyzed and summarized by the Jesuit writer Charles Bent in his book *The Death-of-God Movement*, brought out in 1967 by the Paulist Press, a Catholic publisher.

No wonder the attendance at mainline churches had dramatically decreased! If God was dead, what was the point? (The obituaries of God's death never reached the Fundamentalists, Evangelicals, and Pentecostals, while the Catholics, though their scholars debated the issue, simply carried on as before.)

Rev. Spencer Rice, the Episcopal priest-in-residence at St. John's in Washington, D.C., believes that "our social action exists stronger than our theology today because we don't have any theology anymore—unless you're Fundamentalist or Evangelical and you *do* have theology. In the sixties, social action became a substitute for what had always been the province of religion."

With God buried by American Christian theologians, the religious aid and comfort once based on belief in God that was offered by mainline Protestant ministers to their parishioners seemed to lose relevance, like skills that were no longer applicable, religious versions of buffalo hunting, or lessons in Charleston dancing.

Spencer Rice believes that:

> Personal issues like "How do you talk to someone who's lost a loved one?" "How do you talk to people who are full of fear?" seemed to fade and were substituted by social activism. Social action became a substitute for the historical concerns of the religious community. It's understandable that people who want "real religion" would turn to the Fundamentalists. In the most negative instances, with the absence of a core religious background and feeling, some people have gravitated to what they think is "Christianity" because they hate homosexuals or they've gravitated to "Christianity" for other socially Fundamentalist views, not necessarily religious views. This kind of negative Christianity seemed to be the symbol that scooped all of those people up.

With the "death of God" movement gaining popularity and mainline churches bleeding membership, it hardly occurred to Republican leaders and thinkers (or almost anyone else) after the 1964 election to look to Christianity—or religion of any kind—as the answer to revive their political fortunes. No one thought of Fundamentalists and Evangelicals because no one *ever* thought of Fundamentalists and Evangelicals—except themselves—after they had been erased from the cultural map following the Scopes trial. They had become invisible and they preferred that to being ridiculed.

Republicans were more immediately concerned about the death of their own party than the "death of God" in the wake of Lyndon Johnson's landslide victory and inauguration of the Great Society. "After the Goldwater defeat there was the corpse of organized Republicanism," Bill Buckley tells me:

> and Bill Rusher, the publisher of *National Review*, was very much involved in that aspect of Republican affairs. The head man then was Cliff White, who was primarily responsible for Goldwater's winning the nomination. He was dismissed or, rather, cast to one side when, after the nomination, the Arizonians sort of took over. The consensus of liberal Republicans was that the conservatives, the right wing, had killed the Republican party by getting this man nominated who'd be completely rejected. So our job and Rusher—we were involved completely in the editorial end and Rusher on the organizational—had to go back and talk with these people and say, "No, it wasn't a mistake, it was a historical accident."

I ask if the American Conservative Union (ACU) had anything to do with finding a religious base for the Republican Party.? (The ACU was described by author William Martin in his comprehensive history *With God on Our Side: The Rise of the Religious Right in America* as "a broad-based organization that took care to distance itself from the Birch Society and other elements on the extreme right.") Buckley replies: "Indirectly it did—it was founded in this room."

This room in Buckley's Manhattan town house gives you the sense of being in a womb—warm, cushiony, deep red, with a stunning portrait of a tall, dark-haired woman in a long red gown, who I assume to be Buckley's mother, the grand dame of the clan. "We went down and had a sort of constitutional conference in Washington to decide what should be in the constitution of the ACU," Buckley says:

John Dos Passos was there, and quite a few people carrying a lot of historical prestige. I don't recall any particular talk about enlisting religious groups—the ACU would have been anti–Supreme Court and would have pronounced heavily on any of their decisions that bore on religion. Of course there was the school busing decision and Earl Warren was at very high tide—he was the villain. We had a one-line editorial written by Rickenbacker: "Conservatives are organizing a paean to Justice Earl Warren—they're going to go down to Washington and pee on him."

Buckley gives the trademark Buckley wink. "That kind of slapstick freshman humor somehow works every now and then." He continues:

National Review obviously played a part after the Goldwater defeat, because we had to pick up the pieces. We had to pick up the Goldwater movement and try to rescue it. Teddy White's book on The Making of the President about that campaign was published in the spring of sixty-five and it was reviewed by Ken Galbraith in the New York Times and I think by Pat Moynihan in the *Herald Tribune*. Moynihan said something like: Goldwater lost, he deserved losing, but there were certain things said in that campaign that suggest that the Republican Party is going to be informed by these ideas for a long time. Ken Galbraith said: It's preposterous to assume that there's *anything* of lingering interest in the Goldwater campaign. The miracle, Ken seemed to feel, was that Goldwater wasn't thrown into the nearest ocean and abandoned.

Another Buckley wink, and a smile. "Ken Galbraith is not at his best in prophecy. He'd thought the Soviet Union was going to outpace us economically there for a while."

I ask Buckley, a staunch Roman Catholic, if he'd had any part in the Republicans bringing Catholics and Evangelicals into a political coalition. "No." The answer is so definite and swift that I wonder what Buckley's opinion is of Evangelicals.

"I'm very interested in them," he says, "because it sounds as if they're very unformulated and yet their spirit seems to me quite moving and utterly sincere. I'm at odds with Jeff Hart who, in his history of *National Review*, ends by saying that Bush owed his victory to the Evangelical vote." Buckley's eyebrows rise, as they often did when questioning guests on his TV show *Firing Line*. "Is that true?" he asks me. "Did they vote *qua* Evangelicals?" I tell him that most Evangelicals voted *qua* Republicans.

The '64 campaign seemed to be the definitive conservative Republican defeat of our time—though GOP audiences had been inspired by an actor stumping for Goldwater whose speeches the *New York Times* said had a "moralistic, simplified, and emotional appeal"; but Ronald Reagan declared he was "not a politician."

† † †

The country that slept through the fifties under the soothing leadership of "Ike" Eisenhower was jolted to rude awakenings in the turbulent decade that followed. Young people not only protested racial discrimination in the battle for civil rights, they also protested censorship, the authority of their elders and teachers, the war in Vietnam. The cry of "Freedom Now" was not just for civil rights and free speech, it was also for free love and sexual expression; a whole generation of Americans seemed to have discovered their constitutional right to "the pursuit of happiness," and the chase was on with a vengeance.

"All of that offended people I knew in the South," Joseph Hough explains in his soft Southern accent:

offended them deeply. When the protestors and the draft resisters came, and the sexual revolution, a lot of conservatives who weren't very active became enraged. This stuff was open and blatant—homosexuality, the idea of communes with open sex. They began to associate that with "liberals." In fact it was children of liberals rebelling against their parents, but that's not the way these Southern people saw it. All this was evidence to them that the Gospel they knew needed to be preached with even greater fervor.

The beginning of '68 "started the decline in membership of the mainline churches who supported the civil rights revolution," Joseph Hough points out:

> They were identified with more liberal views, they were more affirmative about the student revolutions going on, and more open in their opposition to the Vietnam War. People were hearing from the pulpit a version of the liberal gospel which worked very well in the civil rights revolution—Christianity, after all, is not only about beliefs in the afterlife but also beliefs about how we should live together in this world.
>
> But what it sounded like to conservatives was that the Church was siding with these new revolutions. Around this time there was an invitation for Angela Davis to speak to a Presbyterian assembly. At that point, organizations like the Presbyterian Laymen in North Carolina began to get organized to stop this move to the left in the Church, and people began to withhold their contributions—some people just left.

This view of the liberal Union Seminary President Joseph Hough is affirmed by the late Diane Knippers, the prominent Religious Right spokesperson who headed the archconservative Institute for Religion and Democracy. Leaders of both liberal and conservative religion agree on one issue—the reason for the fall of the mainline churches' influence.

"A major influence in building evangelical institutions within the mainline churches themselves," Mrs. Knippers told the Evangelical conference in Washington, "was the mainline denominations' move to the left in the sixties. The mainline was truly the mainline in the post–World War II, family-and-church-oriented 1950s."

The backlash over the social activism of mainline churches in the sixties, as well as the whole rejection of middle-class morality and traditional values by the young generation of hippies as they headed for communes, free love, and dope, drove many shocked and disgusted citizens to find solace in the welcoming arms of the Evangelical churches or form conservative groups in their own denominations.

"Goldwater was beaten, so people felt 'Look what's happened—these wild-eyed commies have captured the country.'" Joseph Hough says. "They saw it as communism versus true, virtuous capitalism—and that group began to get upset."

The angry frustration of the Fundamentalist Christians coincided with similar feelings in the ousted Republicans of the Goldwater wing of the party. Young Morton Blackwell, a veteran of the convention that nominated Goldwater, realized that conservative Republicans had no chance of gaining power again unless they could recruit a whole new constituency, a bloc of potential voters who had never been organized and activated. What group of people was angry at the way the society was going and felt left out of it? Blackwell looked upon the Fundamentalists and Evangelicals and saw "virgin timber." Realizing the untapped power of the religious vote, he must have felt like H. L. Hunt when his first oil well gushed, or a nineteenth-century snake-oil salesman watching wide-eyed immigrants getting off the boat in New York.

When Jerry Falwell in 1965 pronounced with piety that "Preachers are not called to be politicians," he was not only attacking Martin Luther King, he was expressing the attitude of Fundamentalists who had simply withdrawn from the society that humiliated them and ridiculed their beliefs after the Scopes trial. If the world saw the fundamentalists as the "boobs" of H. L. Mencken's scathing prose, why engage with the world?

Reverend Mel Schoonover, founder of the Florida Theological Seminary, says:

> The Pentecostals and Fundamentalists developed a scorn of the media and of mainline churches. And they were portrayed in the culture as stupid, as fools. *Apostle* was the first movie that didn't treat these people with contempt. When Republicans paid attention to them, they embraced the Republican Party. It was an affirmation of their visibility and power. They were recognized as an effective force, and it gave them vindication.

Paul Weyrich, like Morton Blackwell, was a young Republican operative who saw potential voters whom others hadn't noticed—in his case it was conservative Christian parents worried about the evils of public schools. Weyrich coined the term "Moral Majority" and helped Jerry Falwell launch his crusade. Weyrich's work was underwritten by the Joseph Coors brewing fortune, which established the Heritage Foundation, a powerful element in the right-wing arsenal. Big money and Republican political strategists lie behind all the Religious Right offensives.

"LBJ's 'Great Society,' Joseph Hough says, "was the most sweeping legislation since the New Deal, done for the least

fortunate part of society. This got another group upset"—
namely, the billionaires, who played a major role in the rise of
the Religious Right.

President Hough remembers that:

> In the seventies, some of the religious conservatives got together
> with people like Nelson Baker Hunt and Lamar Hunt and
> others, and these guys pledged a billion dollars to win the world
> for Christ before the end of the twentieth century. There was
> forged this partnership between the Religious Right and the
> Political Right. W. A. Criswell, the pastor of the First Baptist
> Church of Dallas, was part of it. I was invited by mistake, and I
> didn't go and didn't pay much attention to it at the time, I just
> thought it was a bunch of Fundamentalists. I didn't know these
> guys would become the new Taliban of America.

These billionaire-backed groups, organizations, and foundations abound, all pouring money into the double-barreled cause
of right-wing religion and politics, expressed through conservative Christian churches and denominations and the furthest
right-wing of the Republican Party. The Hunt boy billionaires,
Nelson and Herbert, with other Texas oil barons and fundamentalist preachers, founded the Council for National Policy
(CNP) in 1981. Members include Tim LeHaye, whose wealth
came not from oil but the best-selling Left Behind books, D.
James Kennedy, megachurch pastor and TV and radio evangelist, and longtime Republican operatives Blackwell and
Weyrich. CNP meetings are closed, and no interviews or tapes
of the proceedings are made public, allowing prominent people

in government to speak in off-the-record freedom. Recent speakers at their conclaves include Supreme Court Justice Clarence Thomas and Attorney General Alberto Gonzales.

Jim Wallis says:

> I think the Religious Right is the political seduction of religion. There were political operatives on the far right who had meetings with a handful of TV preachers—and they made a deal—"You give us your lists—your members list, your database—and we'll turn our computers onto your lists, and we'll make you into household names. We'll make you famous and we'll gain political power."

They did; and they did.

† † †

After the big splash that televangelist Pat Robertson made in the 1988 presidential primaries through grassroots organizing, liberals greeted his poor showing in the general election of 1988 with a sigh of relief. Fears that the Religious Right might ever take over America subsided, replaced by that most seductive of all illusions: "It can't happen here."

Liberals laughed or yawned when Robertson predicted in his concession speech that "out of the seeming defeat of my campaign and the demise of what had been called the Moral Majority came an extremely effective force which I believe is the wave of the future, and which is toppling historic liberalism and will bring about a conservative era in the United States."

While the liberal pundits sneered at Robertson's prediction, Vicki Kemper, writing in *Sojourners* magazine, saw that the volunteers who worked in Robertson's campaign "had discovered grassroots politics" and their goal was "to reshape and reorient American politics completely by systematically infiltrating and taking over its basic political structures"—the precinct, country, and state organizations of the Republican Party, as well as local school boards and city and county commissions.

Early the next year, Robertson received an award from a college student conservative group and sat next to Ralph Reed, who had graduated not only from the University of Georgia but also from the Leadership Institute, a training program for right-wing political activists. The institute was founded and run by none other than Morton Blackwell, the Republican Christopher Columbus who discovered fundamentalist voters. Once again, the fundamentalist preacher (Robertson) meets the Republican operative (Reed).

The following September, Robertson called a meeting of his former presidential campaigners and rounded up the usual suspects of the Religious Right, including megachurch evangelist D. James Kennedy and theologian-novelist Tim LeHaye. Robertson also invited Ralph Reed, the bright young man who had sat next to him at that dinner the previous January. Hardly intimidated by the liberals' dismissal of their efforts and their future, the group decided to carry on the work of grassroots organizing, and Robertson decided the right man to lead this new right-wing effort was Ralph Reed. The group didn't even have a name yet but soon became known as the Christian Coalition.

Joseph Hough points out:

When the Christian Coalition got started and hired Ralph Reed, they developed a mailing list which I heard recently is close to thirty-five to forty million people. They organized around school boards and legislatures. In the last eight years these people have become influential far beyond their numbers in the Republican Party and have gained an access to political power and political legitimacy they never had.

That power was a key factor that led to a Republican president, Republican Senate, and Republican House of Representatives in the last election.

By the time Bill Clinton began his first term in office, the Christian Coalition had almost a million members and, along with every other right-wing religious force in America, the coalition set out to damage his presidency. This is what Hillary was mocked for describing as a "vast right-wing conspiracy" against her husband.

That's exactly what it was.

It was also the beginning of what the liberals had assured themselves "can't happen here"—the Religious Right takeover of America, solidified in the reign of George W. Bush.

We're here.

IV.

Invasion of the Leukocytes

In any good strategic planning, the air war precedes the invasion. In the well-planned attack of the Religious Right on the strongholds of liberal Protestantism, the "air war" was waged on radio and television—not only the extensive networks of religious broadcasters nor simply the popular TV shows of Jerry Falwell and Pat Robertson. The most effective and destructive blast came from a nationally influential and purportedly objective source. Only a few in the audience knew that its information had been provided by a new Religious Right organization.

Morley Safer's familiar voice was heard over the heartwarming scene of a Sunday church service in Logansport, Indiana:

This congregation is as generous as any—money to do God's work at home and abroad. But what if some of the money is used to do this man's work?

The bearded face of Fidel Castro appears on the screen.

Or these peoples?

Crowds in Red Square carry a picture of Lenin.

If that surprises you, it may surprise these Methodists even more.

The congregation of the church in Longansport, Indiana, is seen again.

For that act of Christian charity . . . may be the price of a brand-new Soviet assault rifle.

The viewer must surely be shocked—must wonder what unspeakable treachery has deceived the good Midwestern churchgoers into giving (unknowingly) their hard-earned Sunday contributions to buy Soviet weapons for Third World revolutionaries! The revulsion to such a prospect when that segment of CBS's *Sixty Minutes* aired on the evening of January 23, 1983, would be comparable today to showing Sunday donations of well-meaning Christians sent to Osama bin Laden to arm al-Qaeda.

What evil forces did Safer and his *Sixty Minutes* crew courageously expose that night? They painted red the National Council of Churches (NCC) and the World Council of Churches (WCC), the bedrock institutions of mainline Protestantism.

John Wicklein, then associate director for news at the Corporation for Public Broadcasting and a former *New York Times* reporter and editor, explained the animus in an article about the broadcast in *Christianity and Crisis*, the journal founded by Reinhold Niebuhr: "It is true that both councils [NCC and

WCC] characteristically side with the downtrodden and that they conduct programs aimed at alleviating social injustices and correcting human rights violations around the world." Those are the things the right-wingers saw as subversive—the very things the New Testament says that Jesus did.

Wicklein asked the producer of the segment, Marti Galovic, if *Sixty Minutes* had found direct evidence that money from the NCC or WCC had been used to purchase assault rifles for Marxist guerillas. "I didn't try to trace any money for weapons," she said. He asked her if she had gone to Africa to report on the charge that WCC funds given to the Programme to Combat Racism had really gone to support rebel groups in Southern Africa. "No, of course not," she answered.

Safer announced at the beginning of the segment that "One is careful in this kind of report to not make the suggestion of guilt by association, to not use what are generally described as McCarthy tactics." Safer proceeded to do just the opposite of what he said he'd be careful not do, making suggestions of guilt by association that were classic examples of McCarthy tactics. He told the audience that "A great deal of the World Council and the National Council [of Churches] would seem to—not exactly *belong* to the Marxist system, but speak much the same language."

The show was called "one of the most delirious spasms of open red-baiting and intimidation since the McCarthy era" in an article by Alexander Cockburn and James Ridgeway in the *Village Voice*. In a "TV View" column in the *New York Times*, John Corry wrote about the same segment ("The Gospel According to Whom?"): "*Sixty Minutes* never proved that money from a collection plate in Logansport or anywhere else would be used to buy an assault rifle. It was almost as if it didn't think proof was necessary."

Attacks like the one on *Sixty Minutes*, John Wicklein wrote, never had "any solid evidence; never any proof—just accusations and innuendo." Wicklein, who had "over the years done innumerable interviews and background conversations with the leaders and staff workers of these councils," found them "to a person, strongly dedicated to democratic ideals as we conceive them in the West."

While the show was still in production, Wayne Cowan, then the editor of *Christianity and Crisis*, "got wind of the fact that *Sixty Minutes* was planning to do a show on the National Council and the World Council of Churches," and feared what the outcome might be. "At that time neoconservatives were beginning to attack social activism in the Protestant community," Cowan recently explained. He wrote Morley Safer, whom he had met, and expressed his concerns, offering to provide some background information and possible interviewees on the subject with the liberal point of view. Safer never responded.

Frustrated, Cowan decided to try to get the attention of executive producer Don Hewitt by sending a letter to him via his wife, who Cowan knew was an alumna of the Columbia School of Journalism. Cowan recalls that "After Hewitt got my letter, he called to tell me he was mightily offended, that he had forgotten more about conservatives than I ever knew, and that he resented my sending my message via his wife, whom, he said, did not work for the post office." Cowan told him that "from the transcripts I had seen, I could see what they were doing and that if they made no modifications, we would deal with it in the pages of *Christianity and Crisis* when the program was presented." Cowan told me, "For obvious reasons, considering the impact a less-than-twenty-thousand-subscriber publication could have, he couldn't have cared less and plunged ahead."

Twenty years later, Mr. Hewitt was asked by Larry King (*Larry King Live*, December 2, 2002) whether, during the thirty-six years of the show's run, there were any he later regretted. "Yes," Hewitt said, "We once took off on the National Council of Churches as being left-wing and radical and a lot of nonsense. And the next morning I got a congratulatory call from every redneck bishop in America, and I thought 'Oh my God, we must have done something wrong last night,' and we probably did."

A print version of the same kind of attack on the NCC, using the same kind of tactics, appeared in *Reader's Digest*'s January 1983 issue, which dramatically hit the newsstands just before Christmas, in time to scare mainline Christians out of the socks they hung over the fireplace for Santa to fill. The article was called "Do You Know Where Your Church Offerings Go?" with the provocative subhead "You'd Better Find out Because They May Be Supporting Revolutions Instead of Religion."

"Almost always," John Wicklein explained, these kind of attacks "were offered to the press by right-wing fringe groups within and outside the mainline denominations." In the particular cases of *Sixty Minutes* and *Reader's Digest*, the right-wing propaganda passed off as information was supplied by a fledgling group, formed a few years earlier, called the Institute for

Religion and Democracy. The IRD was basically funded by six conservative foundations, mainly the Smith Richardson and the Sarah Scaife foundations, according to an article in the *National Catholic Reporter*. Richard Mellon Scaife, a great grandson of the Mellon fortune founder, transferred grants from his mother's causes of population control and the arts and into conservative groups like the Heritage Foundation. H. Smith Richardson had used the Vicks VapoRub fortune for support of noncontroversial causes such as historical restoration and the Boy Scouts of America, but his son, like the Scaife inheritor, redirected the foundation's money to right-wing groups such as the American Enterprise Institute.

The Minneapolis *Star and Tribune* commented in an editorial after the IRD had successfully launched its double-barreled blast against the NCC and the WCC that *"Reader's Digest* and *Sixty Minutes* uncritically relied upon the Institute [IRD] for much of the information in their scandalous-sounding reports."

The two "conservative critics" used for the *Sixty Minutes* demolition job were Richard John Neuhaus, at that time still a Lutheran minister (he later converted to Roman Catholicism and became a major figure on the Religious Right), and Edmund Robb, an itinerant conservative Methodist evangelist, both founding members of the IRD. The *Reader's Digest* broadside began "with an account of two troubled parents whose children had been asked at Sunday School to collect money for food relief to Vietnam," the Minneapolis *Star and Tribune* noted, going on to reveal that "The article did not mention that the father, David Jessup, was a founder of the Institute for Religion and Democracy. It did find space, however, to print the

Institute's address, along with a five-point list of suggestions from the Institute's chairman for readers who wanted to get involved."

In his own report on the *Sixty Minutes* show, John Wicklein added that "The *Jessup Report,* published privately by the same Mr. Jessup, "contains most of the accusations found in the [*Reader's Digest*] articles, and on the *Sixty Minutes* segment."

Leon Howell, in his informative book *United Methodism at Risk: A Wake-Up Call* reported:

> all these stories had been initiated by the IRD. It had hit the ground running after its 1981 founding . . . IRD was created and sustained with money from right-wing corporate foundations . . . [which] supplied more than 80% of IRD's income during its first decade. From 1981–2001, IRD received about 4.4 million from these nonreligious entities.

The IRD-fed attacks from the *Reader's Digest* and *Sixty Minutes* resulted in a significant lowering of contributions from mainline churches to the NCC, precipitating a decline in the influence of the NCC, which had been identified as "liberal" for supporting the principles and issues of Jesus' ministry: help for the poor, healing the outcasts and fringes of society, and advocating peace and nonviolence.

A report on the IRD had been commissioned by the Board of Global Ministries of the United Methodist Church in June of 1981 because, the board stated in a "Questions and Answers" paper released with the study:

The United Methodist Church has had several attacks and is
aware that the National Council of Churches and other denominations were experiencing similar attacks in publications and
articles sponsored by the Institute for Religion and Democracy . . .
Staff and persons related to the IRD have attended the recent
annual meetings of the General Board of Church and Society and
General Board of Global Ministries [of the United Methodist
Church] and attempted to introduce and influence legislation,
therefore we need to know who these persons are . . . It appears
that the tactics which the United Methodist Church and its agen-
cies are experiencing is a challenge to the order of the Church and
not just a political difference.

The board's study reported that the IRD "was created in
April of 1981 by a group of Washington-based political activists
in conjunction with several conservative Christian leaders who
disapproved of certain social action programs in mainline
Protestant churches." The IRD's purpose, said the report, was
"to develop a political force in a new arena—the religious
world." Part of its stated mission was "to discredit and diminish
the Religious Left's influence in the media." To that end, it had
made a thousand media contacts, including every major religious writer and every religious magazine.

Specifically, this was the start of a self-declared campaign by
the IRD to take over the three largest Protestant denominations
in the United States—Methodist, Episcopal, and Presbyterian—
for the politics and theology of the Religious Right. Continuing
to pour millions into that effort, an IRD funding proposal
in 2000, called "Reforming America's Churches Project:

2002–2004," said that its program "for influencing the governing church conventions of three denominations will cost over $3.6 million over the next four years."

Ed Robb, one of IRD's founders, told an audience in Michigan that "The IRD is giving special attention to reform of the United Methodist Church, America's third largest religious body and the largest denomination under religious left control." The IRD did not have to start from scratch. In the Methodist Church in particular, the seeds of takeover already had been planted. The IRD would nourish them into blooming.

† † †

Charles Keysor, who had served as editor of the Methodist magazine *Together*, that icon of Eisenhower-era, apple-pie Protestantism, started a new magazine and a movement within the United Methodist Church (UMC) called *Good News* in 1967. Its aims were clearly stated when Keysor and his new organization went to the United Methodist General Conference (the national convention held every four years) in 1972 and complained that the Church had emphasized "man's ideas and problems instead of God's truth," specifically criticizing the denomination's support of "women's theology, liberation theology, black theology, Third World theology, theologies of human rights."

Leslie Woodson, chair of the Good News Board of Directors in 1971, praised his troops as "Leukocytes in the Body of Christ—white blood cells fighting to reject an infection." The analogy set the tone for Good News using names of diseases to describe enemies—the majority of fellow Methodist Christians— as "leprosy" and "cancer."

Robert Edgar, head of the NCC, says the right-wing groups within the mainline denominations are:

> like the Commies in the thirties—they're front organizations, working on the inside to get their views adopted. On Justice Sunday, the Religious Right was saying that anyone who didn't agree with their views on the Court was "anti-American." It sounded more like the fifties and McCarthyism.

The anti-American charge has become part of the right-wing religion's standard litany of diatribe. When the Women's Division of the UMC, a favorite target of Religious Right groups, urged the president after 9/11 to use diplomacy rather than war to end terrorism, the president of Good News labeled the statement "virulently anti-American."

Like communist front groups in the thirties, the "leukocytes" in the Protestant churches not only "bore from within" the liberal structures, they also use names that once stood for liberal movements. Organizations within the Methodist Church that ally themselves with the same causes as Good News use the overall term "renewal groups," or "renewal movement," which were once terms for social justice work in the Church.

Even more offensive to mainline progressives is another conservative "renewal" organization calling itself the "Confessing" movement, which historically meant the small minority of Christians in Germany who rebelled against Nazism and called themselves "the Confessing Church." Most famous and revered of that group was the theologian Dietrich Bonhoeffer, who died in a Nazi prison camp before the end of World War II. In an article in *Good News* magazine, a leader of the right-wing Protestant "Confessing" movement compared it to the anti-Nazi Christians who opposed Hitler, claiming that both groups had to battle the authority of Scripture over "alien and humanistic ideologies." The "alien and humanistic ideologies" of the liberal Protestants include women's rights, gay rights, reproductive rights, rights of racial minorities, and human rights.

† † †

The IRD and the front groups like Good News are joined by the National Association of Evangelicals (NAE) in recruiting and converting members of mainline churches to the ranks of the Religious Right. NAE vice president Robert Wenz tells me that part of the NAE's program of "outreach" involves working "to convert members of Methodist, Episcopal, Baptist, and Presbyterian churches into Evangelicals."

At the NAE conference in Washington in 2005, the late Diane Knippers, who had been an IRD board member since its founding, reported:

> I am an Evangelical Episcopalian. In fact, I serve on both the standing committee on ecumenical and interfaith relations for the Episcopal Church and the executive committee of the National Association of Evangelicals.
>
> There are in fact millions of American Christians like me—

Evangelicals who are members of mainline churches. My educated guess is that Evangelicals represent about twenty-five percent of the mainline membership. . . . there is strong evidence that the United Methodist Church is moving in more conservative directions. A major reason is that more conservative regions of the Church are growing—the South, Central, and Midwest regions, while Methodism on the West and East Coasts continues to decline. New formulas allow more representation of these growing regions in Church decision-making bodies. So, in contrast to the Episcopalians, the UMC strengthened its traditional standards on marriage and sexuality at last year's UM General Conference.

The quadrennial UMC General Conference is where the IRD tries to overhaul and undermine the denomination's adopted standards and beliefs. The Methodist Federation for Social Action (MFSA), which began as an early-twentieth-century social justice group led by labor union members and suffragettes, continues that work today. The MFSA sends representatives to the General Conference, opposing the IRD positions and pushing to strengthen the denomination's stand on progressive issues. The Rev. Kathryn Johnson, executive director of the MFSA, says the IRD:

> has an ongoing strategy for the General Conference every four years—they have a sophisticated strategy team and a fair amount of money and resources to put into that. They organize to get folks elected as representatives to the general council, and once they're elected, they have gatherings around the country where

they pay the way for people to come and organize and work with
them. Then they pay their representatives' way to the General
Conference, and they put lots of resources into having them
gather for strategy sessions and meals together. We have far fewer
resources.

When the IRD sends its representatives to those conferences,
they are backed not only with funds but also by, in the warfare
rhetoric of the Religious Right, "Prayer Warriors" at home who
support their efforts. A sample: "Pray that the UMC will break
all ties with the Religious Coalition for Reproductive Choice."
Not all the prayers are so benign—like Pat Robertson's "Prayer
Offensive" against the members of the Supreme Court he
thinks of as liberal, asking God to "make them an offer they
can't refuse" so there will be room for more archconservatives
on the court.

Negative comments are the rule on the Religious Right,
where the still-popular Pat Robertson told his *700 Club* viewers
that "You say you're supposed to be nice to Episcopalians and
the Presbyterians and the Methodists, and this, that, and the
other thing. Nonsense. I don't have to be nice to the spirit of the
Antichrist. I can love the people who hold false opinions but I
don't have to be nice to them."

A nice distinction.

When I spoke to her, Rev. Kathryn Johnson had recently given
a talk on "Laying Down Our Swords within the United
Methodist Church," based on advice from a negotiator of the conflicts in Northern Ireland, who had emphasized the importance of
respect, honesty, and all the right virtues in communicating with

those you oppose. I ask Rev. Johnson how that advice is working out in practice. "I get to test it daily," she says with a laugh. "We get a lot of attacks here, and a lot of our folks who want to attack others." I ask if her attackers were willing to deal on the same terms of virtuous dialogue. "You can't answer generally," she says:

> There are some leaders on the conservative end of the spectrum who are very calculated and working hard to put wedge issues in place to heighten the conflict—but there are many people, maybe including some leaders, who are quite sincere and would be open to looking for common ground. It's a matter of being wise, of not using the destructive attack but being wise—and yet not naïve— in terms of what you're doing. The tragedy is that all this is keeping us back—the more they attack the Church, the more we're in the defensive posture and the harder it is to do what we want to be doing. If they didn't exist, our group would be pushing the Church to convey a vision of where we think the Church should be going. It's hard to do that when we're on the defensive all the time.

NCC director Robert Edgar tells me, "I'm afraid our Methodist brothers and sisters who should be out on the cutting edge are often hesitant because the Religious Right has done such an effective job of dividing, splitting, making accusations, and using language that has been pretty disruptive."

After attending the last UMC General Conference in 2004, Edgar says:

There was plenty of time to talk about homosexuality, internal Methodist business, and little or no time to talk about prison abuse scandals, poverty, justice issues, prison camps at Guantanamo. That group called the Institute for Religious Democracy has been organizing, and they were in full force at the conference, pleased as punch that the conversation lent itself to talk about dividing the Church. I think they would like nothing more than a third of Methodists and a third of Presbyterians and a third of the Lutherans and a third of the Episcopalians all to form a new denomination, based on private piety issues and a narrow set of faith issues.

Jan Love, director of the UMC Women's Division, says the IRD people at the 2004 convention were:

informally floating a proposal for what they call "amicable separation." One of their leaders held a press conference and said, "I think its time for us to separate amicably because we have such profound differences." What they call "amicable separation" everybody else calls schism. The only time there was a schism in the major Methodist family was over slavery in 1844. This is being equated with that.

Rev. Johnson says:

They have a real internal debate—the original founder of Good News left Good News and said "the Methodist Church will never be reformed, we need to break off and form a separate denomination." But they stayed, the majority of them, and they're preparing for both possibilities. For a long time they were setting up parallel institutions that made it look like they were preparing to break off. They have their own mission board, their own publishing house, a separate women's network. They have made the infrastructure to split off, but on the other hand, when they see the possibility that they could actually take over the denomination, some argue that they'd be separating from the resources of the Church if they left.

The way our policy works, if your congregation chooses to leave the denomination, you can do that—but the church building is no longer yours. Some of them are pushing now to change the policy of the denomination so they can split and take their property. That way they'd have the best of both worlds— they don't have to leave the denomination leaving all resources behind. There are articles now on their Web site challenging the policy, saying that should be changed. At various points when they felt successful and strong they felt they could take over the Church and drive *us* out.

IRD leader Edmund W. Robb Jr. said back in 1975 that the United Methodist Church was "sick"—but that "We are dedicated to Evangelical renewal within the UMC. We are not going elsewhere. Rather, we propose to radically alter the direction of our great denomination."

The divisions—not only in Methodism but all the mainline Protestant denominations—are brought about by the Religious Right's use of the "wedge issues," mainly the two major ones— abortion and homosexuality.

V.

The Wedges: Dividing to Conquer

The well-trimmed white beard and the memories of sixties' activism are the only betrayals of age for Harvard theologian Harvey Cox, the best-selling author of *The Secular City* and a shelf of books that includes *Fire from Heaven: The Rise of Pentecostal Spirituality* and *The Reshaping of Religion in the Twenty-First Century*. Cox was one of the activists of the sixties who went South to join the civil rights marches and protests led by Martin Luther King, and one of the Christian leaders, along with William Sloane Coffin and the Berrigan brothers, who protested the U.S. war in Vietnam. Taking a break from his full-time schedule of writing, teaching, and lecturing to talk over coffee in Harvard Square, Cox shares his thoughts about the impact of the "wedge issues" in silencing Protestant progressives.

"The energy of the mainline Protestant churches has been absorbed by the battles over abortion, and over gay rights and gay marriage that's divided entire denominations in recent years," he says. "There's nothing left over for the kind of battles that were fought in the past for peace and justice in the nation and the world."

Jim Wallis, the tireless author of *God's Politics*, told one of his thousand-plus audiences that the Religious Right "created a constituency to turn religion into a partisan wedge—to divide us and destroy us. Religion is not meant to be a wedge that divides us, it's meant to be a bridge that brings us back together again."

That's not the way it's happening, however, in America's churches, where partisans on both sides of the wedge issues cite religious beliefs and quote the Bible to uphold their positions. Within the Methodist denomination, as in most all the mainline churches, "The big wedge issues are abortion and homosexuality," the Rev. Kathryn Johnson says:

> Although the Good News group is consistently conservative on *all* issues, the delegates to the General Conference are overwhelmingly liberal when it comes to other issues like war, or racism, or the death penalty. When it comes to abortion and homosexuality, though, many of them will vote with the conservatives on abortion and homosexuality. We get beat up all the time on our determination that reproductive freedom will have

more legal options rather than fewer legal options. That's tough. Church law says women should have the legal option to make a choice about having an abortion, and that choice should remain available. We have a very carefully nuanced good stand on abortion and the women's division is charged with defending that.

The carefully worded official statement on abortion of the UMC states:

Our belief in the sanctity of unborn human life makes us reluctant to approve abortion. But we are equally bound to respect the sacredness of the life and well-being of the mother, for whom devastating damage may result from an unacceptable pregnancy. In continuity with past Christian teaching, we recognize tragic conflicts of life with life that may justify abortion, and in such cases we support the legal option of abortion under proper medical procedures . . . We call all Christians to a searching and prayerful inquiry into the sort of conditions that may warrant abortion. We commit our Church to continue to provide nurturing ministries to those who terminate a pregnancy, to those in the midst of a crisis pregnancy, and to those who give birth.

The Religious Right groups within the Church respond with their typical rhetoric, like this blast from a group called Lifewatch: "Certain United Methodist leaders and institutions directly collaborated with the culture of death."

Between the General Conferences held every four years there are regional conferences where antiabortion measures are passed in areas where the Religious Right is strongest, such as the South and Midwest. Good News groups and their allies try to build enough support at these localized gatherings to overturn the Church's pro-choice stand at the next national convention. The battle is ongoing. I ask Rev. Kathryn Johnson if the Religious Right is aided by its secular political allies on this issue in particular. "Yes, and its not just coincidental," she says. "There are key overlap people who do political organizing on the abortion issue and are also organizing in churches."

The wedge issues that the Republicans and their religious mouth organs have used to divide the country so deeply and with such destructive rancor—abortion and gay rights—are, not surprisingly, the ones that are most difficult and flammable for the religious/spiritual left to reconcile with the secular left. It is no problem for the two sides that stare at one another without comprehension across the gulf of Belief to agree and join forces on most issues: poverty, the environment, the war, the economy. Yet the sex and reproductive issues are so volatile that failure to express complete agreement on them can mean a hostile dismissal and attack on the dissenter who is in every other way an ally. When it comes to attacking religious progressives on the wedge issues, the secular left can be as vitriolic as the Religious Right.

Jim Wallis told an audience of "spiritual progressives" in July 2005:

> We've had remarkable success on the road, on the book tour, of finding common ground on the issue of abortion. Not common ground that will satisfy everybody on the left and right ends of the spectrum. It satisfies most people in the middle, a lot of

pro-life and pro-choice people. It comes up every single night—
I've actually expanded it from the book because I'm getting a lot
of ideas from people on the road.

It's obvious that one of the ideas he got "from people on the
road" is that legal abortion may be hedged about with qualifi-
cations but cannot be eliminated if you want to find consensus
from a middle-class American audience, including most mainline Christians. Whether or not Wallis ever runs for political
office (and the possibility is not inconceivable), he is involved
with politics and politicians and is trying to have his ideas heard
and make a difference on the national scene. Since his book
became a hit, his advice has been sought by many in government—mainly Democrats—on how to appeal to religious
voters. Hillary Clinton in particular, whom Wallis has known
since 1992, not only has often consulted with Wallis but also
invited him to speak to groups of Democrats in the Senate and
House. Maybe Hillary is advising him as much as he is advising
her, since he has adopted essentially her own policy on abortion:
the ideal number of abortions is zero, but in the meantime, in
Clinton's words, women must have the freedom "to make the
choices that are consistent with their faith and their sense of
responsibility to their family and themselves."
Wallis echoes Clinton as he continues his words on the issue
to his audience of spiritual progressives:

> When it comes to abortion, the place we should start is by talking
> about how to change—dramatically reduce the number of
> unwanted pregnancies. David Saperstein [Director of the

Religious Action Center of Reform Judaism] and I are friends—
he's very pro-choice but he's called for cutting the abortion rate in
half in the next five years. I was with some pro-life Democrats
who want to go further, but they don't want to give up the legal
options—and Hillary is talking about the "tragedy of abortions."

It's hard to know who is influencing whom.

In a phone conversation last summer, Wallis tells me that he
talked with Hillary "the other night," and she said, "She's going
to go further in her stand on eliminating the need for abortions—
not just with words but a kind of 'Prevention First' approach.
She's going to win a lot of people in the middle of the conversation who right now don't like the way the Democrats talk
about it." The issue is sensitive to many Christians who favor
women's right to choice but don't like the harsh rhetoric of
some of the militants.

The Rev. Mel Schoonover, whose ministry has taken him
from the East Harlem Protestant Parish to the founding of
the Florida Theological Seminary, conducts his work from the
wheelchair to which he's been confined all his life. He meets
me for breakfast at a hotel in Miami Beach, a neighborhood
where he has counseled homeless people, junkies, and alcoholics
and was once thrown from his wheelchair and beaten by one of
the men he was trying to help. Rev. Schoonover is still active in
his late sixties as a counselor, speaker, and guest minister.

"Abortion," he tells me, "is the reason the Democrats keep
losing a lot of people. The issue is the right of the mother to
determine what's done in her body. But there has to be a realization the fetus is human—it's not a cabbage. I conducted a

funeral for an aborted child, and it was one of the most serious ones I've ever done."

Rev. Norman Eddy, a prominent East Harlem minister since the 1950s, has written

> Do "pro-life" advocates think life ends with the birth of an unwanted child? What happens to the child of a raped, unwed, teenaged girl? Who puts up the money to have programs for the unwanted children of the very poor, of the addict mother, of the poverty-stricken family? Do "pro-life" advocates care about life after birth?
>
> Do "pro-life" advocates forget that the well-to-do and wealthy were always able to pay a few doctors who will perform illegal abortions? The poor can't afford to pay for an abortion, no matter how desperate the need is for one. So they devise their own horrible methods of trying to create an abortion, some using bent wire clothes hangers. Do the "pro-life" advocates have any answers for caring for the children who are born maimed as the result of botched abortions with wire coat hangers?
>
> Do the "pro-choice" advocates ever confront their "pro-life" opponents with the questions "What are your plans for the lives of unwanted children of the raped teenager, the addicted mother, the poverty-stricken family. Does life end at birth? Doesn't life begin then?"
>
> These are questions from my life experience that don't get asked. The answers to them will affect the lives after birth of countless numbers of babies.

† † †

Debra Haffner, the founder and director of the Religious Institute on Sexual Morality, Justice, and Healing, tells an audience of more than a thousand "spiritual progressives":

> It is time, as Reverend Al Sharpton says, for the Christian Right to meet the right Christians. And, I will add—the right Jews, Catholics, Buddhists, Pagans, and Unitarians. We need to challenge the moral vision of the Right, we need to ask, "Is it ever moral to coerce a woman into carrying a pregnancy to term? Is it ever moral to deny young people lifesaving information?"

Haffner is a trim, dark-haired woman with clear-rimmed glasses who is also the minister of the Unitarian-Universalist Church of Westport, Connecticut, as well as a wife, the mother of a college student, and the author of books such as *From Diapers to Dating*. She meets with me in the restaurant of the Lombardy Hotel in Berkeley, California, where we've both come to this "Conference of Spiritual Progressives" sponsored by *Tikkun* magazine. Haffner is here to speak and to chair a workshop on sexual issues, and I'm here to interview progressive leaders like herself.

Haffner grins as she tells me, "People laugh when I say I am a minister and a sexologist—it seems like an oxymoron, like 'Jumbo shrimp.' " No one laughs, though, when they know her work, whose pinnacle has been the seemingly impossible task of creating a "Religious Declaration on Sexual Morality, Justice, and Healing" that has so far been signed by more than 2,400 religious leaders, representing forty different faith traditions, from forty-three states and twelve countries.

Haffner explains:

I got five of the leading theologians in this country to come together in a room and I said to them, "All of you write books, and I need four hundred words from you." My whole career has been spent trying to translate difficult issues into ways that America will go "Oh—I get that," so, we did. It took a year. It started with three days together but it took a year, with a total of twenty high-level theologians and denomination leaders all concurring.

This is the result:

Sexuality is God's life-giving and life-fulfilling gift. We come from diverse religious communities to recognize sexuality as central to our humanity and integral to our spirituality. We are speaking out against the pain, brokenness, oppression, and loss of meaning that many experience about their sexuality.

Our faith traditions celebrate the goodness of creation, including our bodies and our sexuality. We sin when this sacred gift is abused or exploited. However, the great promise of our traditions is love, healing, and restored relationships.

Our culture needs a sexual ethic focused on personal relationships and social justice rather than particular sexual acts. All persons have the right to and responsibility to lead sexual lives that express love, justice, mutuality, commitment, consent, and pleasure. Grounded in respect for the body and for the vulnerability that intimacy brings, this ethic fosters physical, emotional, and spiritual health. It accepts no double standards and applies to all persons, without regard to sex, gender, color, age, bodily condition, marital status, or sexual orientation.

God hears the cries of those who suffer from the failure of religious communities to address sexuality. We are called today to see, hear, and respond to the suffering caused by violence against women and sexual minorities, the HIV pandemic, unsustainable population growth and overconsumption, and the commercial exploitation of sexuality.

Faith communities must therefore be truth seeking, courageous, and just. We call for:

• Theological reflection that integrates the wisdom of excluded, often silenced peoples, and insights about sexuality from medicine, social science, the arts, and humanities.
• Full inclusion of women and sexual minorities in congregational life, including their ordination and the blessing of same sex unions.
• Sexuality counseling and education throughout the life span from trained religious leaders.
• Support for those who challenge sexual oppression and who work for justice within the congregation and denomination.

Faith communities must also advocate for sexual and spiritual wholeness in schools, seminaries, and community settings. We call for:

• A faith-based commitment to sexual and reproductive rights, including access to voluntary contraception, abortion, and HIV/STD prevention and treatment.
• Religious leadership in movements to end sexual and social injustice.
• God rejoices when we celebrate our sexuality with holiness and integrity. We, the undersigned, invite our colleagues and faith

communities to join us in promoting sexual morality, justice, and healing.

Haffner says, "Within two months I had eight hundred and fifty people who endorsed it, and we ran it as a full-page ad in the *New York Times*. Since 2002 I've been building a network of religious leaders who are willing to speak out on sexual justice issues."

Haffner's work involves teaching people that sex and spirituality are neither antithetical nor even incompatible, as they are usually regarded in American culture, but are actually desirable partners. "Our work is really twofold," she says:

> one is to help congregations and denominations deal with the sexuality issues of people they serve. Our slogan is "Pastors for Sexual Health, Prophets for Sexual Justice," so another part of our mission is to engage a prophetic voice on a broad range of sexuality issues.
>
> There are thousands, if not tens of thousands, of religious leaders out there who understand and are committed to this issue. The history is long—Tom Davis did a book called *Sacred Work* that traces the history of clergy involvement in Planned Parenthood. With Margaret Sanger's work, it was the clergy who were able to get birth control into New York City hospitals starting in the 1940s. There is in America a long, strong, committed history of religious leaders speaking out about women's rights to their body; more than that, the history of prosexuality voices go back before Scripture. As a sexologist, when I was in seminary, I had to take all this Christian history, which frankly,

as a Jewish Unitarian, didn't hold a whole lot of interest to me, so I said to my history professor, "I'm having a hard time with this," so he said, "What do you want to learn about?" and I said "sexual politics."

I studied all the documents of the Church Councils, and almost every council from 325 to the 650 had a piece on sexuality issues. They talked about who could marry who. When Augustine said, "Virgins are better than married people," a man named Jobenia said and Junia of Aquina said, "That's not true at all—didn't Paul tell you that 'As to virgins, I have no specific information from the Lord.' " The problem is, we have lost much of this—but people don't remember Martin Luther said clergy could marry—he'd fallen in love with a nun, and his own experience of what the sacred was in terms of sexuality in interpersonal relationships was too real for him to walk away from it.

† † †

Debra Haffner's coleader of the workshop on sexuality at the Conference of Spiritual Progressives is Rev. Ignacio Castueras, the pastor of St. John's United Methodist Church in the Watts neighborhood of Los Angeles.

The author of *Dreams on Fire*, a collection of sermons given after the Rodney King riots in Los Angeles, Castueras also holds a position I was not aware existed—and it didn't exist until he saw the need for it and convinced others of its value—he is the first national chaplain of Planned Parenthood of America. A short, congenial man who speaks with passion on issues that concern him, he's a Mexican-American whose mostly African-American parishioners support his national work with Planned Parenthood.

I meet with Castueras at a small square outside a Berkeley church where his sexuality workshop was held, and we talk as people pass around us, some sitting down with a sandwich for lunch. Speaking about abortion issues in his own Watts neighborhood, Rev. Castueras says, "The African-American community is now dealing with the issue of sex education and abortion much more creatively, thanks to the work of the Religious Coalition for Reproductive Choice."

It was started more than thirty years ago:

The original name was the Religious Coalition for Abortion Rights, but blacks and Latinos were reluctant to join an organization that had "abortion" right up there in the name. When the name was changed eleven years ago, it became more focused on African-American churches.

There's a Sexuality Summit at Howard University, now in its seventh year. Statistics are still high for unmarried African-American getting pregnant, but they are going down, unlike in the Latino community, where it's really a major problem. There needs to be a Latino Sexuality Summit.

We're on the progressive edge now. The African-American minister James Forbes of Riverside Church in New York was at our meeting of Planned Parenthood this year, the annual interfaith prayer breakfast, and he spoke about "Choice." We can still talk with our more conservative colleagues in the Latino and African-American communities about sex education, if not abortion. We say, "Come to the table to talk about education, about the availability of contraception—if you don't want to talk about abortion we don't have to talk about abortion. Let's talk about these other things." I've had success with that approach even among Roman Catholics, and most of pastors in those churches, they have to look the other way.

† † †

At the last General Conference of the Methodist Church, the forces of "Good News" scored their most significant victory in tightening the denomination's rule on homosexuality. Rev. Kathryn Johnson of the Methodist Federation for Social Justice explains:

The basic legislation on this was passed in 1972, with the sentence "Homosexuality is incompatible with Christian teaching." That sentence was simply put in—it was added to social principles which are for guidance—not the law—of the Church. Every four years since then negative stuff on homosexuality and positive things have been added to it. There are positive things like protecting the civil and human rights of gay and lesbian people, that they shouldn't be discriminated against, that they are "sacred people of worth." Also every four years there have been more restrictions added, like United Methodist money can't be spent at the national level to promote homosexuality. That clergy can't perform holy unions of gay and lesbian people, that such unions can't be offici-ated in our churches, no ordination for homosexuals: "Self-avowed practicing homosexuals cannot be ordained" and then it was added "and also may not be appointed." Folks on the left keep finding loopholes and folks on the right keep coming back and closing them.

Jan Love says:

At least half of what Good News put forward at the General Conference failed, probably the majority of it. One was on attacking the women's division, one was on more stringent doctrinal requirements for the ministry. The one they got was on homosexuality, where the rules were tightened. There were openly gay or lesbian pastors in our denomination who had been through trials and been acquitted, by finding loopholes in the rules. The UM position had been that you can be gay but you can't act on it—but these ministers have committed relationships, so that's proof they are acting on it.

Part of the provocation was the Massachusetts law that was passed allowing gay marriage, and open gay weddings in San Francisco. These things gave rise to extreme worry on the part of the people who wanted to make sure gays and lesbians are not ministers.

Many of our gay and lesbian clergy were asked to leave, and many left on their own steam who didn't want to go to trials. I'm convinced we're losing a lot of members because of it. I know of cases where a local church in one community has become so conservative, some people left. A woman who left one of these churches said she took it as a bad sign for the denomination.

There's [the] Reconciling Ministries Network trying to convince the Methodist Church to be a welcoming church for gays and lesbians.

Rev. Ignacio Castueras, pastor of the Methodist church in
Watts, tells me:

> No matter what the General Conference says, we as a congre-
> gation are going to offer you your rights and our rites. There
> are more than four hundred Reconciling Congregations or
> ministries across the nation—some are campus ministries,
> some are churches. We will get there, just as the UCC has
> done.
>
> The gay issue is divisive in all our Methodist churches, not
> just the African-American and Latino. We're working in sort
> of a pincers movement—getting more and more local congre-
> gations to become "reconciling congregations"—meaning open
> and accepting of gays. And we will keep on working on it leg-
> islatively every four years at the National Conference.

The Reconciling Ministries Network in fact became the hot
issue of the day for the IRD when the gay group held a conference called Hearts on Fire on the Labor Day weekend of
2005 at Lake Junalaska, a United Methodist retreat center in
North Carolina. For the weeks following the conference, the
IRD Web site home page was full of stories on protests against
the group and against the Methodist-operated retreat center for
allowing the group to use its facilities. The IRD was joined in
its protests by, of course, Good News, the group it supports
within the Methodist Church, as well as other "Renewal"
groups and their allies, such as the conservative Southeastern
Jurisdiction of the UMC, as well as the Baptist Association of
Haywood County, where Lake Junalaska is located, and the

Ku Klux Klan. The IRD was quick to try to disassociate itself from "the nefarious racist group."

IRD spokesman Mark Tooley wrote a diatribe against the use of the Methodist conference center by the progay Reconciling Ministries group, and another Religious Right group, the American Family Association distributed it. The sentiments expressed in Tooley's article evidently fit right in with the Ku Klux Klan's own policies of hate and discrimination, so they posted it on their official KKK Web site. Tooley, embarrassed by the obvious "guilt by association" practiced so often by his own group, wrote to the Klan demanding that they remove his article from their Web site. He received the following answer from the Imperial Wizard of the American White Knights of the Ku Klux Klan: "The Christian thing for you to have done was to ask yourself if contacting me in the manner that you have [asking that his article be removed from the KKK Web site] would make you a hypocrite."

It's a question that participants in the Hearts on Fire conference might well have endorsed.

The conflict around the issues of homosexuality and religion is affecting every Christian denomination, most of all the Episcopalian. The Reverend Spencer Rice at "the Church of the Presidents" in Washington, leans back slightly in his chair, contemplating the issues of sexuality that drive the "wedges" into current religious life:

> Christianity has affixed herself to these social issues that have been here forever. The homosexual issue is, in terms of the Episcopal Church, more important than race was, more important

than women priests, more important even than abortion. There's almost nobody who doesn't have a passionate point of view on homosexuality, one way or the other.

Rev. Rice expressed his own view on the most divisive issue in the Episcopal Church—the ordination of the first openly gay bishop in the denomination's history in 2003. Rev. Eugene V. Robinson's ordination as bishop of New Hampshire by a confirmation vote of sixty-two of the 107 bishops (a simple majority was needed to confirm) was strongly protested by Bishop Robert Duncan of Pennsylvania, who said in behalf of those opposed that "This body has denied the plain teaching of Scripture and the moral consensus of the Church throughout the ages . . . May God have mercy on this Church." Bishop Duncan said he was "filled with sorrow" and felt "a grief too deep for words."

Rev. Rice comments:

I am not an enemy of the homosexual community, and I know the homosexual community by having been a minister in San Francisco for twenty years. The bishop of New Hampshire fell into a trap that I think the homosexual community often falls into. They put their homosexuality out front and say, "If you can deal with this, you can have access to me." I don't care if a person is a homosexual, bisexual, heterosexual, or any other kind of sexual, but when they do that, in my judgment, they're lost. They're making their sexuality the primary issue of the interpersonal, and I think that has cost the Church dramatically. It's not going away.

Even the abortion issue is not as inflammatory. I've been watching the homosexual issue grow in the country and in the Church for the last forty years, and it's the most inflammatory issue I know of. People who don't give a hoot and a holler about almost anything else in our society have a view on homosexuality. I think the issues of homosexuality and abortion will continue. I don't think they can be put to bed by the Archbishop of Canterbury or anybody else.

Neither did Diane Knippers when she spoke at the NAE conference in Washington in March of 2005 and traced the loss of membership in the Episcopal Church in 2003 to the appointment of the openly gay bishop. Knippers said the "sudden 2003 dive [in Episcopal membership] is most likely found in the controversy over the new homosexual bishop consecrated in the fall of 2003. Indeed, schism in the worldwide Anglican community affecting the Episcopal Church remains a likely possibility from this extraordinary event."

The Episcopal Church lost 36,000 members in 2003; the previous year's loss was 8,000, whereas a slight growth was seen in the years prior to that. The Church pointed out that all Protestant denominations were declining, attributing it to factors such as "a decline in the birth rate among white, highly educated Americans" and "losing more to the 'nones'—the disaffiliated population, which has affected all denominations, but the mainline more than anybody else." Declining average attendance in the Episcopal Church was reported for the third straight year in 2005, but, according to Rev. Charles Fulton, director of congregational development, "does not appear to be primarily linked to fallout from the 2003 convention," when the gay bishop of New Hampshire was ordained.

From such statistics, sociologists, journalists, and laypeople—including progay and antigay activists—will draw their own conclusions.

† † †

Gay couples hugged and sang "Amen" at the 2005 General Synod of the United Church of Christ when an "equal marriage rights for all" resolution was passed, while other delegates stormed out of the Georgia Convention Center predicting a schism in the progressive denomination. The *Atlanta Journal-Constitution* reported that "Some members fear the issue could tear denominations apart much like slavery did in the 19th century." While the Methodist, Presbyterian, and Episcopal churches are struggling over what has become the hottest-button issue in American Protestantism, the 1.6-million-member UCC became the first mainline denomination to endorse gay marriage.

Before the end of the year, in their Southern Conference several UCC churches had voted themselves out of the denomination over the gay marriage issue. An opposition group out of Texas called the Evangelical Association began several years ago to recruit conservatives in the UCC churches, using similar tactics as Good News does to divide the UMC. Unlike the "renewal" movements in the other mainline churches, however, the Evangelical Association does not want to take over the UCC but only secede from it and set up its own churches. Some of the UCC churches in the South, in the midst of Baptist churches and conservative communities, were ripe for revolt.

Rev. Julie Peeples, minister of the UCC's Congregational United Church of Christ in Greensboro, North Carolina, whose own church is one of many "Open and Affirming" congregations in the denomination, is disturbed by the actions of dissidents in other parts of the state. She reports:

> One pastor in North Carolina was voted out of his church through an effort led by several individuals who were coached by people allied with the Evangelical Association, and two more ministers in two separate churches returned home from trips out of town to be informed their congregations had called meetings and voted themselves out of the denomination without the ministers' knowledge.
>
> There are regular meetings of the Evangelical Association, and workshops offered to help disgruntled members "educate" the rest of the congregation on the "evils of the UCC" and how to leave it. There is a system of "moles" who are coached in tactics such as getting themselves on key boards and committees, and getting by-laws changed so that they can try to keep the Church property if they leave the denomination.
>
> In some cases there have been personal vendettas against the pastors [who supported the gay marriage resolution], including, in some cases, [against] their families, hoping to drive them out. One minister was voted out who was only six months from retirement and now will not get the pension or health insurance he would have received from the denomination. The people behind all this are heartless.

I ask if she sees any chance of the gay issues being resolved in a decade in the way that the women's issues were resolved in the seventies. "The opposition people say they feel even stronger on this one," she answers. "They say 'We gave in on integration, we gave in on women's ordination, but we can't let this happen, or scriptural teaching falls apart, Christianity falls apart, society falls apart.' This is where they draw a line in the sand."

The UCC's efforts to be inclusive have also met with opposition outside its own ranks. The denomination launched a campaign called God Is Still Speaking, with a powerful promotional commercial that shows a gay couple holding hands as well as African-American and Latino people being turned away from a church. People of all races, genders, and ages are shown entering a UCC church with the message, "Jesus didn't turn people away. Neither do we." The ad was turned down by CBS and NBC on the grounds that it "raised controversial issues." It ran on ABC Family, CNN, BBC, Discovery, Hallmark History, and other cable channels.

The other mainline "progressive" denomination, the Unitarian-Universalist Association (UUA), is overwhelmingly "humanist" rather than Christian and has ordained gay ministers for several decades, including the popular lesbian pastor of one of its historic flagship churches, the Arlington Street Church of Boston. Christians compose only 10 percent of the UU, while assorted brands of humanism, from Pagan to Zen make up most of the denomination.

The UUA minister Debra Haffner expresses the most optimistic outlook for acceptance of gays in America's mainline churches:

We're the first denomination where half the clergy are women. In the seventies we saw a rapid change in women's ordination. None of the denominations had been ordaining women, and some of them who had been ordaining women—like the Unitarians in the 1800s—had stopped ordaining them. Between 1970 and 1979, every major denomination changed its policy. If you go back and look at the Episcopal Church on women's ordination—it was bloody. People said they were going to leave, they lost churches, they took away the standing of the first bishop who ordained a woman, said it was an illegal ordination; but by '79 all the denominations but the Southern Baptists had women clergy. That movement was hard, and people struggled against it, and ultimately people knew that women deserved to be religious leaders. I think we are very close to entering that point of gays and lesbians in the Church—that the denominations are ripping themselves up over it, having these big fights, but you know people forget—the reform Jews have prosexuality policies on all this stuff, UCC does, UU does. The three big mainstream Christian Protestant groups—Methodists, Presbyterians, Episcopals—have all been struggling with this, and the votes have been really close.

The Episcopals will lose some churches over this, but they lost churches during slavery, and during the ordination of women. You know there's a Gay Pentecostal Alliance—there's not a religious body that does not have a group working for sexual justice, for sexual minorities. I think that's where we are now. I really believe that in ten years every denomination, with the exception of Southern Baptists and Roman Catholics, will affirm the rights of gays and lesbians. I also think that most Western countries will

have same-sex marriage in ten years, including most of the
Eastern and Western states in the U.S. The middle of the country
may take longer, but it will happen, just as it did with interracial
couples. Maybe I'm just an optimist, but I do believe Martin
Luther King's words that the "arc of the universe bends toward
justice."

With a practical as well as positive message, Haffner sees
hope for the coming of sexual justice for all. She tells the audience at the "Spiritual Progressives" conference:

> We need to remember that the vast majority of Americans sup-
> port what we support: family planning, sex education, an end to
> discrimination in sex education—and 62 percent of Americans
> support marriage or civil union for gays. We need to understand
> that America supports the right to privacy. In the third presiden-
> tial debate, even George W. Bush said, "Consenting adults can
> live the way they want to live."
>
> Actually, I knew this was public opinion more than a decade
> ago when mattress discounters bought a full-page ad in the *New
> York Times*. The ad showed two people cuddling in bed—it was
> impossible to see the sex or gender of either of the bodies, or if
> either had on a wedding band. The tagline of the ad said: "Who
> you sleep with is your business—how you sleep is ours. Call 1-
> 800-MATTRESS."

VI.

Megachurch Meets Mainstream

Jennifer Hearn's mother had been asking her to go to church with her sometime. Ms. Hearn, an elementary school teacher in the Earlington Heights Elementary School in Liberty City, Florida, went to her mother's flourishing church, the Coral Baptist Church in the Glades in Coral Springs, Florida, one recent Sunday morning. This is how she described the experience:

> "Looking for a sign from God?" the sign said. "Well, here it is . . . Coral Baptist Church." The parking lot was brimming with SUVs and minivans, and there were still more arriving. The

architecture of the church was of the same ubiquitous Suburban South Florida–style that creates visual patterns when driving on the highway. It is as though the identical sand-colored concrete homes with orange-shingled roofs somehow coalesced into one God-sized structure. When we walked in the entrance of the church, the ambiance changed dramatically. It was dark, cold, and it smelled musty. I was emerging through something ethereal. A cloudy substance, like mist or fog, was enveloping me. Was I feeling the spirit of God, like my mother had described to me when I was younger? We sat down somewhere near the back, and my senses began to explore. I discovered the fog machine behind the stage that was giving me that mystifying feeling: a simulacrum of spirituality. There was a man on the stage who was reading announcements in a jovial Southern accent, "encouraging" us to do this and "encouraging" us to do that. This was certainly different from what I heard in school as a child. I never felt encouraged, only threatened.

The lights dimmed, and an opaque blackness fell upon us like a starless night. A light-green phosphorescence in the shape of a cross began to illuminate the alcove behind the stage. Suspended from the darkness, the cross revealed the galvanized eyes of the congregation. A man's gentle voice seemed to dissipate the darkness as the lights from the ceiling began to softly glow, and the cross once again faded into the whiteness of the alcove. The voice was speaking intimately to Jesus, but in a way that somehow included hundreds of people.

He said "Amen," which was echoed by the ricocheting "Amens" from all over the church in voices that were young, old, male, and female. The lights were turned on to their full brightness, and the chords of an electric guitar cut through the recent and uni-fied sentimental feeling. For the next fifteen minutes, a rock 'n' roll band performed Cat Stevens covers, with modified lyrics that glo-rified Jesus. A strobe light projected long pink tentacles that played on the congregation. The lyrics were projected on two large movie screens over a backdrop of psychedelic images that moved kaleido-scopically. They reminded me of some paintings my husband showed me that some of his friends sent him from Peru, depicting hallucinations induced by Ayahuesca, a native plant that shamans take in order to reach spiritual enlightenment.

When the music was over, the lights once again dimmed and the phosphorescent cross was resurrected. The sounds of thunder crashing silenced the energy that resonated in the amphitheater-like space, and formidable lightning bolts, the color of purple veins, lit up the two movie screens. Then a voice, low and omi-nous, filled the room with a rush of cold air. "The perfect storm," it said.

When the lights came on again and the cross was once again camouflaged in the whitewashed walls, Pastor David Hughes was sitting on a stool in the middle of a stage, wearing baggy blue jeans and a faded navy-blue T-shirt. He had charisma that I have never seen in a preacher, and a persona so unpretentious that he did not even speak behind a pulpit. He gave a lighthearted sermon about Moses (whom he referred to as "Mo") leading the Israelites out of Egypt. He re-created the story, omitting the archaic biblical language and replacing it with modern-day collo-quialisms. The Israelites would address "Mo" as "Dude" and "Man" in their complaints. "Dude," they would whine, I told you we should have stayed in Egypt!"

I opened a calendar I picked up on the way out. There is an event every night of the week. The programmatic quality of the church gives it the "something for everyone" appeal, from drama lovers to single moms. It is a department store for blessings.

Welcome to the megachurch, America's fastest-growing religious facility. Unlike traditional, mainline Protestant churches that used to be the backbone of all-American, middle-class Christianity, most megachurches are informal in dress, in speech, and in their religious message, and highly sophisticated in marketing. Sunday services can sound and look more like rock concerts as parishioners in jeans, shorts, and T-shirts dance in front of their seats in the big auditoriums to Christian rock, and at youth group sessions Christian teenagers move to the beat of Christian hip-hop. Psychedelic lights and fog machines can create their own altered states, which pass for religious experience.

Alongside all this is the old traditional "Little Church around the Corner," with an opening hymn like "Lead Kindly Light, Amidst the Encircling Gloom" sung to organ music by robed choirs and mostly lip-synching parishioners made up of men wearing suits and ties and women in dresses and sometimes even hats, followed by prayers and Scripture read in a monotone from a program, and a sermon on the discipline required to follow Jesus, given by a gray-haired man in a black robe—the whole experience may seem more in tone and mood like a funeral service.

Lee McFarland, the unordained minister of Radiant, a megachurch in the fast-growing town of Surprise, Arizona, expressed the vision—as well as the lingo—of his kind of religious institution when he told people as the church was being built that he didn't plan on having stained glass or a steeple: "We want the church to look like a mall—we want you to come in here and say 'Dude, where's the cinema?' " Sticking to the theme, Radiant boasts a drive-through latte stand and serves Krispy Kreme doughnuts at Sunday services. As McFarland told *New York Times* magazine writer Jonathan Mahler, "I'm just trying to get people in the door." According to Mahler's article "The Soul of the New Exurb," McFarland was getting 15,000 in the door. And counting.

While the megachurch phenomenon was looked on with pride by the Evangelicals, with discouragement by the mainline, and as the latest hot religious story of 2005 by the media, a perceptive dissent came from Alan Wolfe, professor of political science and director of the Boisi Center for Religion and American Public Life at Boston College. Professor Wolfe, author of *The Transformation of American Religion*, wrote that the Evangelical megachurch displays such "strong a desire to copy the culture of hotel chains and popular music that it loses what religious distinctiveness it once had." Wolfe believes that "there is increasingly little difference between an essentially secular activity like the popular entertainment industry and the bring-'em-in-at-any-cost efforts of evangelical megachurches."

At least one megachurch skipped the arduous process of constructing an imitation mall that would draw people in who were looking for a cinema, and simply took over a cineplex. In Waterville, Maine, the former local movie mecca is now the Faith Evangelical Free Church, and on its marquee, which once showed film titles, there are megachurch-spirited messages: "Is Your Tank Empty/ Spiritual Fill Up—Here"; "Our Price Hasn't Changed in 2000 Years."

The Web site of the Saddleback Church in Forest Hills, California, flashes images of young couples with children, a pair of pretty young women, an Asian man and boy, people greeting others with outstretched hands. Everyone is smiling. A generation ago, the promotional photos on the Web site might seem to an observer like advertisement for a country-club-type resort, but certainly not a *church*. Such an impression might certainly linger on entering a Sunday service, when rock music comes from five singers, two electric guitars, a drum set, an electric keyboard, two saxophones, a piano, a trombone, a trumpet, and a flute, with a light show flashing over it all and attractive young women dancing and singing onstage.

The pastor, Rick Warren, is the Evangelical flavor of the day, whose book *The Purpose-Driven Life* has not only stayed on bestseller lists but has become the handbook of a movement of ministers who have taken his workshops on *The Purpose-Driven Church*, the title of his first book. The 20,000 people who attend one of the four services on an average Sunday are not only entertained by the music and concert camaraderie that results in shouts of "Jesus rocks!" but they are also taught, in everyday-language sermons, the bedrocks of conservative belief. The church's statement of "What We Believe" includes "The Bible is the perfect guidebook for living . . . Heaven and Hell are real places . . . Jesus is coming."

In the meantime, Warren is backing up his "purpose-driven" rhetoric with action. After Warren's Saddleback Church fed homeless people in Orange County for forty days, he asked his congregation, "So you did it in Santa Ana, don't you think you could do it in Uganda?" *Christianity Today* reported that Warren is trying a new approach to church humanitarianism. Rather than collecting money to send to professionals, "he wants to directly link local churches to churches overseas."

† † †

Robert Wenz, vice president of the National Association of Evangelicals, tells me, "There are now 850 megachurches in the U.S., and they are predominantly Evangelical."

Not all bear the denominational name of "Evangelical," but even if they don't, they may be one of the predominantly Evangelical churches within another denomination. Megachurches are defined as those with an estimated 5,000 members, or an average Sunday attendance of 3,500, but they are organized into small "cells" or groups of ten or twenty members who meet regularly to pray together and discuss personal concerns and goals. "The key to the megachurch," says Wenz, "is to get people into some sub-group where they connect with people and are ministered to in their personal life. It keeps the church from being intimidating. And there are groups in these churches for every concern. If you have acne, there's probably an acne support group."

Nearly all the growth of the megas has taken place in the past two to three decades, according to a study by the Hartford Institute for Religion Research. These churches with gigantic congregations are found everywhere in the United States but are mainly concentrated in Florida, California, Texas, and

Georgia. Some of them even have spires, though not always in the old traditional manner.

The first time I spotted the towering main building of the Coral Ridge Presbyterian Church from the highway northwest of Fort Lauderdale, I thought I might have taken a wrong turn and wandered onto Cape Canaveral; the imposing structure pointing to the sky with a needlelike spear or spire resembled a missile-launching site. It was actually the central building of Coral Ridge Presbyterian Church, one of the oldest mega-churches, founded in 1960 in an elementary school, moved to its new megabuilding in 1973, led by Rev. D. James Kennedy, a prominent and influential figure on the Religious Right. Kennedy was one of the first ministers to introduce political issues into his sermons both at church and on his growing television and radio network back in the seventies, and was one of the original board members of Jerry Falwell's Moral Majority when it was founded in 1979.

An SUV in the parking lot conveys the spirit of the place with a bumper sticker that says "I Care Not for Kerry—Bush '04."

Unlike Rick Warren, the popular Hawaiian-shirt-sporting minister of Saddleback Church, Rev. Kennedy wears the traditional black robes with red collar trim and is backed not by a rock group but a monstrous silver-pipe organ with surely enough pipes to blow a missile skyward and a massive choir in traditional blue robes belting out the old familiar hymns, like "Immortal, Invisible." There are a number of gray, or white, or bald heads in the crowd, and men in suits with ties and women dressed up, a few even with hats. A roving camera scans them for the television transmission of the service.

In the pulpit, Rev. Kennedy (A.B., M.Div., M.Th., D.D., D. Sac. Lit., Ph.D., Litt. D.Sac. Theol., D. Humane Let.) leads the Lord's Prayer and then poses a question to the congregation, "What would you do if you knew you couldn't fail?" He goes on with variations on wanting what we can't have, knowing what we can't get, which seem to lead to a murmuring confusion in the congregation, until he stops and says, "I'll put it another way—what would you do if you had an assurance of success? You do—by God." He reminds us that we have dreams as children, but alas, we grow, "and then a pesky voice says that we can't, that we never could, that *you can't, you can't, you can't.* Then he whispers *"These are the words of the Devil."*

He proceeds to tell a story about a man who got fired from every job he had in his teens and his twenties, and continues to get fired throughout his thirties and forties. "And when he reached his sixties, this man received a social security check from the government." Rev. Kennedy does not explain how this man got a social security check if he never held a job, but this is a sermon, not a high school class. No one raises a hand to question. Kennedy goes on spinning his story, telling how this hapless failure of a man blamed all his bosses, and decided at sixty that he'd become his own boss. He gave himself the title of Colonel and invested all his money (I wondered if his money came from accumulated severance pay) in a chicken stand. The business grew, with more and more stands in more and more places, until it became the largest fast-food chain in the world.

The punch line: "Colonel Sanders continued to thrive for twenty more years."

A young man sitting next to me leans over and whispers to

his Latino girlfriend, who hasn't been able to follow all the English. "*Pollo*," he says. She wonders why the minister is talking about chicken, but he tells her to shush so he can hear the rest.

The minister tells all the retired people they could learn from Colonel Sanders, though instead of urging them to start their own new business, he says "I know one man—*one man*—who single-handedly brought 867 people into the church." In the last five years, Rev. Kennedy says, "Coral Ridge evangelism [this includes the TV and radio networks] has led sixteen million people to Christ worldwide."

The congregation applauds.

"In another ten years," Rev. Kennedy goes on, "I project 250 million people will find Christ, and this blows my mind." He rubs his forehead and continues. "If you extrapolate another decade, one billion people worldwide will be won to Christ."

He cites other examples of "Can-do" and "Can't-do" attitudes, and leads to St. Paul, "who said he could do all things *through Christ*." He emphasizes this does not mean "PMA—'positive mental attitude' or 'positive thinking,'" which goes only so far "because it is a sin," this wiping out the teachings of Tony Robbins and Norman Vincent Peale in one swoop.

On another Sunday, a darker side of the uplifting message of the church is glimpsed when Rev. Kennedy issues a warning to all who are present. Before the congregation can take part in their communion service—partaking of the bread and wine that symbolize the body and blood of Christ—the minister makes clear that not everyone is welcome to join in this ritual, and there are dire consequences for those not qualified. "This is a church we want you to participate in," Reverend Kennedy says:

> The whole world is invited to partake of all the things we offer except one—the Holy Eucharist, communion. This is *only* for those who are members of this family, who have been born into the family of Christ, whose hearts have been changed, who have been given the blessed assurance of everlasting life. All others are forewarned, lest they eat or drink damnation unto themselves. Many who have done this become sickly, or weak, or sleep. There are indeed *tombstones* that say: "He partook unworthily of the supper of the Lord and was not saved."

In other words, if you are not a Christian—by *our definition*—and you presume to eat this bread and taste this wine, you will get sick or die. Different churches, even sometimes within the same denomination, have different rules and standards for who is invited to take part in the communion service. Although I have taken communion as a guest at Glastonbury Abbey, a Benedictine monastery in Hingham, Massachusetts, I was told by a priest at the Paulist Center in Boston (both these facilities are Roman Catholic institutions) that I was not welcome to partake of their service. "Communion," he explained, means "community," and since I was not part of that community of faith, it was not appropriate for me to take communion there, unless it was "a spiritual emergency." He did not indicate how such an "emergency" might be determined (I wondered if the situation had to be described and perhaps go as high as the Vatican to be ruled a "spiritual emergency"), but at least he didn't threaten me with illness or death if I swallowed the thin wafer or took a sip of the wine.

Religious Right groups brand any faith that sanctions choice for women in reproductive rights as being part of "the culture of death," but they seem morbidly inclined toward death in their extremism, their vigorous support of the death penalty, their endorsement and support of the U.S. war in Iraq, their fondness for using the language of war and battle in their own righteous religious campaigns that they carry into politics and culture.

I am a Christian but I don't belong to Reverend Kennedy's "family in Christ," so I didn't dare stay for communion. I left the main church to go into the bookstore, where I found Rev. Kennedy's views expressed in a number of books, perhaps most clearly in *The Gates of Hell Shall Not Prevail: The Attack on Christianity and What You Need to Know to Combat It*: "We are called to be soldiers of Christ" and "to bring all of creation under His control. It is the marching orders of the Army of Christ. If we claim to be soldiers in that army, then we are under orders to do all we can to bring this nation back to God." Scripture teaches us, writes Kennedy, that "a faithful Christian must be involved in the political and social issues of his or her time."

Kennedy and his fellow soldiers of the Religious Right like to quote a passage in Genesis (1:28) that says "Then God blessed them and said to them, 'Be fruitful and multiply, fill the earth and subdue it; have dominion over the fish of the sea, over the birds of the air, and over every living thing that moves over the earth." Kennedy then adds his words to God's words, interpreting the above passage: "This mandate includes the federal government."

Nowhere in the Bible could I find the words "federal government."

What Kennedy means is that he is twisting the Genesis creation story to the Religious Right political agenda, meaning that they who claim to represent God on earth—or anyway, in the United States—must approve elected officials. As he puts it, "Those that would flaunt their disregard for moral and ethical standards [determined by him and his like-minded colleagues] will find it increasingly difficult, and finally impossible, to be elected to high office in this nation."

Sound pompous and overblown? Well, almost a decade before the first two presidential elections of the new millennium, Kennedy predicted that "in the twenty-first century, Evangelical Christians will be the dominant force in elections in this nation."

Here's another "biblical principle" as interpreted by Kennedy: "God commands men to form civil governments to stem the growth of violence by administering the death penalty." Huh? Where is this? Kennedy cites Genesis 9:6, which says "Whoso sheddeth man's blood, by man shall his blood be shed: for in the image of God made he man."

Huh? How did we get the death penalty out of that? Besides, if you want to get biblical, Kennedy is quoting from the first book of the Christian Bible's Old Testament; what about the New Testament and the teachings of Jesus, who told us to love our enemies and turn the other cheek?

As in most of Religious Right Christianity, the heart of Jesus' teaching is ignored.

To justify war and support for war, Kennedy performs
another of the yogalike gyrations the Religious Right practices to
twist the basic message of Christianity from love to hate, from
the Christian nonviolence that Martin Luther King practiced to
lead the civil rights revolution, to the bloody and ravaging war
in Iraq of the Bush administration. Kennedy says the New
Testament "call to repentance did not demand men to leave the
sphere of military and political activity, but only to conduct
themselves in such offices in a just manner." This he gets out of
Luke 3:14, which is not even spoken by Jesus but by John the
Baptist before the coming of Jesus: "And the soldiers likewise
demanded of him, saying And what shall we do? And he said
unto them, Do violence to no man, neither accuse any falsely;
and be content with your wages."

In Pastor Kennedy's theology, "Do violence to no man"
somehow comes out as a justification for the slaughter of thousands in a war of invasion.

On and on go the distortions that comprise the "theology" of
the Religious Right, twisting Christianity into a creed for violence and intolerance. They not only twist biblical passages to
come out with different, sometimes opposite meanings, they do
the same with the English language. "Tolerance," for instance,
has become a bad word for Rev. Kennedy and his colleagues.

An entire two-sided page of instruction in the new "tolerance" (which is similar to the old intolerance) is available from
another of the Coral Ridge Ministries' programs, the Center for
Reclaiming America. "Fast Facts: Tolerance" features a quote
from Ryan Dobson, author of *Be Intolerant* (who could have
predicted this title pushed as a "Christian" book a generation

ago?): "Tolerance is the virtue of those who believe in nothing. Rather than stand up for what is right or wrong, the voice of tolerance says we should just let everyone be, that we'll better understand each other if we accept them as they are." A whole new book promoted in the Reclaiming America flyer is called *The New Tolerance*, and its author, Josh McDowell, is quoted on the new, distorted understanding of the word: "True compassionate love that seeks to provide for and protect another person's health, happiness, and spiritual growth could not comply with the cultural call: 'If you love me, you'll endorse my behavior.' Because real love—true love—grieves over the inevitable results of wrong behavior."

And who's the judge of "wrong behavior"?

It is not Jesus, who told "those without sin," to "cast the first stone"—no, it is the rigid Religious Right enforcing their campaign against gays, women who choose abortion, doctors who perform them, nonbelievers, believers of another faith, or Christians who follow the teachings of Jesus rather than the teachings of Jerry Falwell and Pat Robertson, Bill Frist, and George W. Bush. It is for this reason that the Religious Right campaigns against hate-crime legislation; it curtails their diatribes and misinformation about gays and lesbians, pro-choice women, doctors and clinics, those who oppose the war in Iraq, or indeed any part of their agenda.

Coral Ridge Ministries' "tolerance" instruction gives an example of the kind of tolerance they oppose: West Palm Beach mayor Lois Frankel agreed to fly a gay rights flag over City Hall because one of her goals as mayor "is that all these diverse people be able to live and work and play together."

Woe unto her!

The Coral Ridge Ministries' Reclaiming America encourages its members to get active in community and politics, instructs on how to get out the vote and how to run for school board and local offices, and opened a Washington office "as an outreach to Capitol Hill." The D. James Kennedy Center for Christian Statesmanship gives local Bible studies for Capitol Hill staff and provides "Evangelism Explosion" training.

Reclaiming America gives instruction to church members throughout the nation on "How to Motivate and Train the Members of Your Church to Effectively Impact Your Community" by becoming a "church liaison"; suggestions for activities include "Hold a voter registration drive," "Promote election day," "Understand the law" ("be informed about tax exemptions for churches and ministries"), "Network with local ministers."

The liaison information from Reclaiming America goes on to ask, "What issues concern you? Is it abortion, the liberal media, pornography, homosexuality, the public school system, family values, the movie industry, or our local library? Choose one or two that you believe you can address effectively with the help of other citizens . . . Don't wait—get started now!"

The "outreach" of the multimillion-dollar Coral Ridge Ministries is as much political as it is religious. Its influence is indisputable. *The Coral Ridge Hour* airs on more than five hundred TV stations, three cable networks, and three satellite networks. Rev. Kennedy's daily half-hour radio program is heard on over five hundred outlets across America and his three-minute daily commentary is on some three hundred radio stations.

In his latest "outreach" campaign, Rev. Kennedy is pictured holding the lower jaw of a mammoth that was said to roam the earth during the post-Flood Ice Age. Beside him is Tom DeRosa, executive director of the Creation Studies Institute (CSI), who is holding a large bone of a different shape, the femur of one of those roaming Ice Age mammoths. Always on the cutting edge of the religious/culture wars, Kennedy's Coral Ridge Ministries has teamed up with CSI in "a national creation outreach . . . to defend and promote creation and to expose the lie of evolution."

"There are groups in power in this nation," Rev. Kennedy said, "who have a vested interest in promoting evolution." He neglected to mention that they are called "scientists."

Episcopal bishop John Shelby Spong, in one of his newsletters on the Internet, answered the question from a reader from Kansas who asked if "Intelligent Design" being debated by the Kansas Board of Education was "just another way of bringing in conservative belief about instant creation." Bishop Spong replied:

> On one level it really doesn't matter what the Kansas Board of Education thinks, evolution is real and is not subject to majority vote, any more than whether epilepsy is caused by demon possession . . . The pursuit of knowledge should never be compromised to protect religious sensitivities. That is where religious tyranny begins.

Science, however, is not the basis for the CSI, whose mission, according to Mr. DeRosa, is "to bring people to Christ through the message of Creation. When people see the Creator God they can be brought to Christ."

The fossils of mammoth bones said to be found from three to four thousand years ago around some rivers of Florida are supposed to prove that the earth is only six to ten thousand years old, the theory of "Young Earth Creationism" that calculates the earth age at six to ten thousand years by adding up the life spans of Adam and his descendants. Source: the book of Genesis. Most scientists believe the earth is billions of years old—but then, they didn't use Genesis for their studies. The fossils are called "dinosaur bones" by the CSI.

The CSI has been around for seventeen years, but now the new vogue of Intelligent Design being pushed by the Christian Right has given it new publicity, attention, and support. Quick to see its potential for pushing this latest part of the Religious Right agenda, Rev. Kennedy is building a museum called The Creation Discovery Center on the ground of the Coral Ridge church. The *Miami Herald* reports that the museum will display "exhibits on Noah's flood, The Ice Age, and the dinosaurs (featured in the antediluvian room in a mural with Adam and Eve)."

To instruct young people in this approach, the CSI offers Ice Age Fossil Floats, billed as:

> a family-centered activity in which one is taught how to collect and interpret Florida fossils using a biblical framework. Several floats are scheduled each year (Spring and Fall seasons) on the Peace River in Arcadia, Florida. Throughout the weekend, the guests enjoy not only the river float and fossil hunt, but also a fun

fellowship social, a barbecue dinner, an interactive show and tell, campfire fellowship and a worship service/Bible study.

Kool-Aid is not mentioned, but may be optional. Like the Coral Ridge Ministries of D. James Kennedy, the Religious Right megachurches meld their religious messages with politics, and were ripe for GOP plucking in the 2004 presidential election. In his *New York Times* Magazine piece on megachurches, John Mahler reported that the Bush campaign's liaison for social conservatives, Gary Marx, "went directly to megachurch pastors, not for endorsements, he says, but to encourage them to help get out the vote." The Republicans concentrated especially on young, middle-class couples, and "megachurches were a key part of the strategy."

During the campaign, Bush seemed to be running for the office of America's minister rather than its president. In the Coral Ridge *Communicator*, a publication of James Kennedy's megachurch, a page on prayer carries a picture of George W. Bush and this quote from the White House:

I am inspired, uplifted, and comforted by the fact that millions of our fellow citizens whom I will never know actually take time to pray for me and Laura and our family, for which I am eternally grateful. It's an amazing country, when you think about a country that prays for its leaders, regardless of their political party. It's an amazing country, and I can't tell you how grateful I am, and how touched I am, and humbled I am by this—the outpouring of prayer by fellow citizens.

† † †

The Christian mainstream is still with us, their faithful treading water and trying to stop the drain from their denominations while fending off attacks from Evangelical torpedoes and the drift into unbelief and indifference.

The Evangelicals, buoyed by their own success and growth in numbers and political influence, watch with relish the demise of their fellow Christians in the mainline churches. "By the middle of the next century," megachurch pastor James Kennedy predicted in 1996, "most of the mainline churches in America will have disappeared. I predict that the historic 'mainline churches' will be discovered to be 'back alleys,' 'dead-end streets.' "

The late IRD leader Diane Knippers relegated the mainline to "the 'sideline,' or the 'old-line' " when she spoke at the 2005 NAE conference in Washington.

Mrs. Knippers described the mainline churches as:

those historic Protestant denominations that represented mainstream American religion for most of our history. These are the venerable "downtown" churches, the ones located on Main Street in our towns and cities. While no longer representing a majority of American Christians, they still boast prestigious universities and theological schools and are still disproportionately represented among American elites in business and politics, and, to a lesser degree, in academia and communications . . . the 8.2 million United Methodist Church, the 5 million–member Evangelical Lutheran Church in America, the 2.4 million–member

Evangelical in America, and my own 2.3 million-member Episcopal Church.

"Every year brings reports of membership declines. In the ten-year period from 1990 to 2000, the Lutheran Church in America declined 2.2 percent, the Episcopal declined 5.3 percent, the American Baptist Churches declined 5.7 percent, the United Methodist 6.7 percent, the Presbyterian Church declined 11.6 percent. During this time, the U.S. population increased by over 13 percent. Growing churches, by and large, were more conservative . . . The growing churches in America are attracting immigrants, younger people, the unchurched, and yes, some of the former members of mainline churches.

It's not only the Religious Right that recognizes the mainline decline—the bare statistics prove that it's true, and mainline leaders are disturbed, perplexed, and trying to buck the downhill slide. "Those sociologists who told us in 1958 in Santa Barbara that the mainline would recede and the Evangelicals grow, understated the case," says the Episcopal reverend Spencer Rice. "When I became confirmed in 1942 there were four and a half million Episcopals in the U.S. Now we have 2.2 million. I see Christianity at the present time in a very confused posture."

Rev. Mel Schoonover, the Union Theological Seminary graduate who founded the Florida Theological Seminary, says:

The mainline Protestant churches have lost their large presence —their headquarters are all having trouble. There's a disintegration of mainline congregations. There's the lack of an idealized reason or for denominations existing separately, aside from brand-name loyalties and ministerial pension funds. Many of the new megachurches have no denomination.

Liberal Christians need to go back and look at Scripture. Their religious rhetoric is tired and stale, not interesting. They won't have an effect unless they go back to Scripture and tradition. What is the authentic voice of our religion? How does it guide us? The UCC and UUA are playing on inclusiveness as their image— including polyamorous, all sexual expressions—but what are you including us *into*? Their worship is not very exciting.

Rev. John Buchanan is minister of a mainline church, the Fourth Presbyterian Church of Chicago, whose size and attendance would rank it among the megachurches. He believes the decline of the mainline churches:

> is more sociological than theological. These mainline denominations are old, their churches are in old neighborhoods. Many of these new Evangelical churches are more flexible than we are, they're not "real-estate-locked" like the Presbyterian Church USA is. These old churches of ours are in old neighborhoods, and they're dear places—I'm not proposing we shut them down, but they're not going to catch fire and turn into big churches anymore.

Rev. John Buchanan says of his prospering Fourth Presbyterian Church that:

> We're bucking the trend—we continue to grow pretty steadily. We're about 5,300 members. No, I wouldn't say we're a

megachurch. We don't have a coffee bar and a restaurant and health club and that kind of stuff. What we have focused on is mission, worship, and educational programs for our members. Those are our specialties.

Perhaps the biggest appeal of Rev. Buchanan's church is that he has always made it "purpose-driven"—even before Rick Warren wrote his best-selling book on how to do it. "We invest a lot of energy and creativity and a lot of money in mission to the city," Buchanan explains:

> We think that's pretty attractive to a lot of people—they want to belong to something that makes a difference. They want their religion to "walk on the street." We have a full-service social service center that deals with the indigent, the homeless, a counseling center, a tutoring program for kids from the Chicago Housing Authority, a day care center, a health center that serves most members and also needy people in the neighborhood—it's a whole constellation of programs.
>
> We try to create opportunities for our guests and our neighbors and our members to be together. We have a Sunday night supper that's essentially to provide food for homeless people who have no food, but we make sure that church members come to it, and talk with them so we have a sense of one community.
>
> I think we're an example that membership loss does not have to do with theological position whether you're left, middle, or right. I think the other side would like us to believe that mainline denominations lose members because they've become too liberal—it's more complicated than that.

Yes, it is more complicated, and one of the sources of the complication—and a problem for the mainline that is seldom acknowledged—is the difference between the effect of "liberal religion" politically and "liberal religion" theologically. Most often the two have gone together in the white Protestant churches, though rarely in the black churches, which are overwhelmingly conservative theologically and liberal politically.

Rev. James Kennedy analyzes the downfall of the mainline churches as "those that have, by and large, become liberal [in theology], while seminarians turn out ministers who do not believe in the Bible—the kinds of ministers . . .who don't believe Jesus said three-fourths of what is attributed to him and now reveal they don't even believe that He rose from the dead."

Rev. Kennedy's case against liberal theology strikes at the cause of the weakness of Christian belief in mainline Protestant and even some current Catholic theology.

Never mind rising from the dead—according to John Dominic Crossan, a Roman Catholic priest and theologian—Jesus didn't even perform any miracles. In his book *Jesus: A Revolutionary Biography*, Father Crossan argued that Jesus, heretofore famous for his healing of lepers, blind men, and at least one madman (one who was "possessed by demons"), didn't literally heal anyone. Crossan wrote that Jesus was "healing illnesses of people" in a psychosocial sense but not "curing the disease" in a biological sense.

Crossan is part of the Jesus Seminar, a group of scholars and theologians working to determine the historical facts of Jesus' life by voting with colored tiles on what passages of the Gospels are true, not true, probably true, or doubtful. My fellow Christian

Reynolds Price, the distinguished novelist and professor of English at Duke University, says of the Jesus Seminar, "It is really sort of touching and amusing to see them trying to apply scientific method to human history—or take the hopeless stand that if you can't prove Jesus said so-and-so, then he didn't say it. How are you going to prove what was said two thousand years ago?"

Nevertheless, that is the "liberal theology" (as opposed to "liberal politics") that has influenced most mainline ministers. Many of them take the work of the Jesus Seminar as—well, it's hard to resist saying—they "take it as gospel." This leads to the problem H. Richard Niebuhr (the brother of Reinhold and a noted theologian in his own right) was talking about when he mockingly defined liberal religion as "A God without wrath brought men without sin into a kingdom without judgment through the ministration of a Christ without a Cross." Biographer and historian Warren Goldstein says that Richard Niebuhr told another historian "he regretted that sentence more than any he had ever written." But he did write it, and it does stick.

Mark Lilla, in the *New York Times Book Review*, wrote: "The more the Bible is treated as a historical document, the more its message is interpreted in universalist terms, the more the churches sanctify the political and cultural order, the less hold liberal religion will eventually have on the hearts and minds of believers." In *The Chronicle of Higher Education*, Warren Goldstein responded: "I read that sentence to a group of retired Baptist, Episcopal, Presbyterian, and UCC clergy members the next day. They had been reflecting on their long careers, many of them proudest of their dissenting roles in society; they were rightly offended by Lilla's rhetoric."

But they were of the Martin Luther King generation, the William Sloane Coffin generation—the last generation of mainline Christian activism. Goldstein and those retired ministers were talking about their accomplishments in *liberal politics*, not the "liberal theology" that Richard Niebuhr and Mark Lilla are talking about. And it's more difficult for ministers and churches to get people to go beyond themselves, to risk themselves, to devote themselves wholeheartedly to a cause for the rightness of the cause without the belief Dr. King had in the Jesus of the Gospels rather than the historical Jesus who may or may not have said or done what historians and theologians may or may not agree he said or did.

The more that time passes, the more it seems that mainline Protestantism reached its peak of passion and activism in the civil rights movement not only because of the political message of Dr. King but also because of the religious faith of King and his African-American followers. Somehow, it was alright for buttoned-down white Protestants to shout "Amen" and clap and move to the rhythm of black hymns being led by black ministers and their congregations in the cause of civil rights, though it would have seemed, well, a bit "over the top" to act that way in your own Episcopal or Methodist or Presbyterian church back home, where moderation, modesty, and monotone delivery are the standards of religious behavior. What a thrill it was, how goose-bump-producing, to sing "We Shall Overcome" at the top of your lungs, holding hands at an integrated worship or rally and swaying to the music, as if you believed not only in the cause but also in the God and the Jesus of Martin Luther King. The memory of it was maintained by many white activists who went on to protest the war in Vietnam, and then the music faded, and the memory of it was no longer enough.

Even some college-educated white mainline Protestants could believe King himself when he said that after the black children were killed in the church bombing in Atlanta, he prayed to know if he should continue his work if it was going to lead to the death of children, and he said he heard the voice of Jesus, who told him to go on. Would the scholars and theologians of the Jesus Seminar consider that true, not true, probably true, or doubtful?

VII.

Taking Back the Faith

The monologue of the Religious Right is finally over and a new dialogue has just begun.

—Jim Wallis

S hades of the sixties! There's a rally taking place on the steps of Sproul Hall at the University of California at Berkeley, the legendary site where the student firebrand Mario Savio lit the flame of the "Free Speech" movement that helped give the flower-power decade its image as the era of youth and rebellion.

It's forty-one years later, though, and the gathering crowd is not as large, as raucous, nor as young as the ones that grabbed the headlines and attention of the nation and even the world four decades ago. Men with white beards and young mothers pushing baby strollers stop to listen and hope for inspiration or simply to find out what's happening. The speaker is no eager sophomore warning his comrades not to trust anyone over thirty but a somewhat portly middle-aged man wearing a dark-blue suit (necktie stripped off for action) and a blue-and-white yarmulke, talking about (who could have believed it four decades ago, when God was officially pronounced dead?) a *spiritual* crisis! The speaker, however, is neither unfamiliar nor ill at ease with the place where he stands and its significance.

"The first time I ever spoke in public was in this building on December 2, 1964," Rabbi Michael Lerner reveals to the crowd. The founder and editor of the magazine *Tikkun* (a bimonthly Jewish and interfaith critique of politics, culture, and society) and founder and rabbi of Beyt Tikkun Synagogue in Berkeley, Lerner remembers how:

> I led a Hanukkah service at the sit-in for Free Speech at 1 A.M. in the morning, and two hundred of us out of the eight hundred of us in this building came to Hannukah service, lit the candles, and sang. At that moment there was the possibility of a unification of a spiritual voice with a political voice.
>
> I was president of the Berkeley SDS—Students for a Democratic Society—and my experience was that if I wanted to be taken seriously in the liberal-progressive world, I had to go back into the closet with my religion and spirituality. It wasn't, by the way, non-Jews who were doing it to Jews; lots of Jews were saying "Forget it, keep that religious stuff out of it," and Christians were saying the same thing.
>
> My experience on the left was that on Shabbats I could go to synagogue but I sure couldn't tell that to any of my comrades in the movement, who thought it was fundamentally irrational,

stupid, and had nothing to do with what they were about. We've seen that dynamic play out over the last forty years and it has led to a left that has left itself behind, a left that has not been able to connect to the deep spiritual hungers of the American public. As a result, we've lost politically, and we have to stop that. It's important to us not just to say "There's a spiritual crisis," but to understand what that spiritual crisis is—and to turn it around.

Michael Lerner's return to the steps of Sproul Hall four decades after his first initiation into politics was brought on by the (dare I say) "spiritual" as well as political depression suffered by half the country when they awoke to George W. Bush's renewal of power in November of 2004—power to wage war abroad in whatever country he chooses to demonize and at home against the economic interest and welfare (as well as the civil liberties) of all but the society's wealthiest citizens. For people whose faith is mocked and besmirched by the warlike, jingoistic rhetoric of the Religious Right, it is all the more dispiriting to realize that such sacrilege disguised as Christianity has aided and abetted the extension of the Bush Brigade's power to wage war not only against Iraq but also against the American middle and lower economic classes.

Waking to the postelection hangover of November 2004, Rabbi Lerner called his assistant, Robyn Thomas, and simply said, "We've got to do something."

By "doing something," he meant something more than writing, speaking, and setting up Web sites. He meant taking the sort of action the Republicans started engaging in after the Goldwater defeat in 1964: organizing. Lerner wrote an editorial in his magazine on "The Need for a Spiritual Left," and began planning "a five-day national interfaith gathering on spiritual activism" in Berkeley in July of 2005. Lerner and his staff built a program for it, featuring nationally recognized Protestant mainline, Evangelical, and Roman Catholic as well as Jewish and secular leaders, from Episcopal bishop John Shelby Spong to physicist Fritjof Capra, and, even more than anticipated, in the field of spiritual politics as well as baseball dreams, "they had come."

Registration for the conference had to be closed a few weeks before its opening day on July 20 when it reached 1,300, the capacity for the space that had been reserved in the University of California's Pauley Ballroom and in halls and rooms for talks and workshops in meeting sites around the neighborhood. On opening night, the ballroom is packed to capacity with a crowd whose enthusiastic response gives evidence to Lerner's contention that "there's a hunger out there," which his co–keynote speaker, the Evangelical progressive Jim Wallis affirms: "People want to join something, they want to be part of something — they want to make a difference."

There are evidently many people like the nurse from Santa Cruz who I meet while taking BART back from Berkeley after the opening night. I ask how she had heard about the conference. "I got something in the mail about it," she says. "I don't even know how. I saw the words 'spiritual' and 'left' and decided to come."

Buoyed by the overflow crowd and enthusiastic response of the night before, Lerner is no less impassioned as he speaks to the casual lunchtime crowd on the steps of Sproul. Calling for a "Spiritual Left" in this country, Lerner argues that:

liberals, trapped in a long-standing disdain for religion and tone-deaf to the spiritual needs that underlie the move to the right, have been unable to engage these voters in a serious dialogue. Justly angry at the way that some religious communities have been mired in authoritarianism, racism, sexism, and homophobia, correct in their determination to not allow the right to impose their variant of religion on the rest of us under the guise of making America a Christian nation, the liberal world has developed such a knee-jerk hostility to religion that it has both marginalized those people on the left who actually do have spiritual yearnings and simultaneously have refused to acknowledge that many who move to the right have legitimate complaints about American life.

It was not only as a student at Berkeley that Lerner learned he had better check his spiritual talk at the door if he wanted to be taken seriously by liberals and intellectuals. He described the deeper desires of the American public for what he called "meaning needs" and spelled out their importance in *The Politics of Meaning*, a book that caught Hillary Clinton's attention in President Clinton's first year in office. Rabbi Lerner was invited to the White House to discuss the subject with the president and his wife, who felt it was not only interesting but significant.

When the media heard that such a touchy-feely notion as "meaning in politics" was being taken seriously in the White House, predictable howls of derision and catcalls of contempt were heard throughout the Beltway. Rabbi Lerner was labeled a "guru," a term always garnished in the media with standard sneers and jeers. Discussing politics and "meaning" with a rabbi seemed as far out to capitol reporters as holding séances with Madame Blavatsky in the Lincoln Bedroom. Lerner's moment faded, along with the ideas he was trying to pitch to the Democratic Party—ideas that were sorely needed in their clueless 2004 election campaign.

Perhaps to assure potential allies among the spiritually allergic that his movement was not out to brainwash, convert, or otherwise taint their unbelief, Rabbi Lerner makes clear that "We are not advocating that people on the left should all become religious or spiritual. What we are advocating is a left that is friendly not only to secularists and militant atheists but also to people of faith who share a commitment to peace, social justice, and ecological sanity."

As part of his call for such a coalition, Lerner winds up with a twist that points his own compass farther to the left than most of his secular liberal critics:

> If you progressives would get over your ferocious antispiritual and antireligious anger, you'd be able to discover what we knew from the moment we started *Tikkun* more than eighteen years ago: *that the spiritual crisis [in the United States] is rooted in the dynamics of capitalism and can only be healed by a fundamental transformation of the economy and political structures that govern our world.*

I doubt that the Rove-Bush-Cheney team and their religious disciples will recognize that message as "spiritual."

Lerner's friend and fellow keynote speaker, the maverick evangelical Reverend Jim Wallis, joins him now on the steps of

TAKING BACK THE FAITH 159

Sproul. When Lerner presents him to the outdoor crowd, there is clapping, whistling, and shouts of support between sandwich bites from conferees who have spilled out from Pauley onto the sidewalk with box lunches they've bought for $7 ($5 for vegetarian, because "vegetables cost less") and want to hear again the speakers who inspired them the night before. The baby boomers in attendance get the added nostalgic buzz of being at an outdoor protest rally on the Berkeley campus again. All that's needed is Bob Dylan's singsong chant in the background that something's happening and you don't know what it is, do you, Mr. Jones?

Lerner turns over the microphone to the white-haired man in a black suit and starched white collar beside him who could pass for a priest (he'd be good casting for the Bing Crosby role in a remake of *Going My Way*) but in fact is the evangelical minister Jim Wallis, whose TVQ (recognizability rating on the tube) has risen dramatically since pushing his best-selling book *God's Politics* on Jon Stewart's *Daily Show*. Wallis says he knows fame has struck when a young desk clerk recognizes him from the late-night hit and gives him an upgrade at a Comfort Inn outside Detroit.

I have heard mainstream leaders call Wallis "a prima donna" and Lerner "a problem guy" in terms of working with other groups, but with their own followers and most audiences, they are charismatic and effective, and so far they've been able to work with each other.

Like Lerner, Wallis founded and edits his own liberal religious magazine *Sojourners*, which was "progressive evangelical" in politics and theology before most Americans were aware there was even such a category; and like Lerner, he has worked on issues of poverty and the economic interests of workers for more than two decades. Wallis "walks the walk" not only in his work but also when he walks down the streets of the poverty-stricken and blighted Columbia Heights district of D.C., the neighborhood where he lives with his second wife and their six-year-old son.

Lerner started the Institute for Labor and Mental Health, which morphed into *Tikkun* magazine and the Tikkun Community, a network of subscribers devoted to the same causes who try to meet and exchange ideas and programs in their own communities. In 1995 Wallis began his Call to Renewal program, a national federation of churches, denominations, and faith-based organizations from a spectrum of theological perspectives to campaign, organize, and raise money to fight poverty.

Shortly before the Berkeley conference, Wallis organized and led a group of U.S. religious leaders to lobby for world poverty relief at the G8 economic meeting in Scotland. Wallis will organize a group of coreligionists to support or protest an issue at the drop of a hat and fly with them to exhort political leaders to "do the right thing." On the eve of the Iraq invasion, he organized a group of American religious leaders to fly to London to meet with Tony Blair and present him with a letter signed by all of them to appeal for a halt to military plans for Iraq and to support the United Nations' effort to resolve the issue of the weapons of mass destruction that were never found. President Bush, the self-advertised Christian, refused to meet with these religious leaders opposed to invading Iraq—no doubt he was too busy praying for guidance from Jesus, his "favorite philosopher."

Like Wallis, an early opponent of the war in Iraq and a rebel within his own faith community, Lerner works for peace in the Middle East by supporting the rights of the Palestinians as well as Israel, a stand that earns him the enmity of a large sector of American Jewry. Robyn Thomas, his willowy assistant for the last four years, says, "I've never known anyone who's had as many death threats as Michael—though I seem to be catching up."

Politically and professionally, Lerner and Wallis seem to be almost mirror images, and they've developed a kind of stage patter that warms up an audience. It's easy to imagine them as a pair of theological song-and-dance men or stars of a "spiritual sitcom," a kind of clerical version of *The Odd Couple*, with Lerner as the disarrayed Oscar Madison and Wallis as the smooth Felix Unger. Surely such a hit would spawn spin-offs and perhaps even popular ethnic stories ("a rabbi and an evangelical go into a bar. . .").

Lerner and Wallis first became aware of each other through their magazines, which Lerner describes as "parallel to one another," and they met when Wallis invited the rabbi to speak at a conference of his antipoverty Call to Renewal movement. They had dinner at each other's homes, but really got to be friends when they were both arrested, along with a group of thirty or so others, in the Rotunda of the U.S. Capitol in a protest against the government cutting taxes for the wealthy and at the same time cutting programs for the poor (a political approach that now seems standard).

"They left us in handcuffs on the bus we'd come down on for

about six hours before going to jail," Lerner recalls, "so there was plenty of time to talk."

"In the D.C. jail," Wallis adds:

> There was Tony Campolo, a Baptist evangelist, and Rabbi Michael Lerner, having a theological argument about "Who was Jesus Christ—the son of God or a prophet or what?" They're friends, but they were really going at it, and watching them I got it—this is the way you do interfaith work—you all get arrested for your faith, and talk theology in jail.

Wallis has perfected his book-tour oratory (today's version of the nineteenth-century "stump speech") with the smooth flow of long-practiced preaching to win and hold a crowd, assuring these listeners that:

> Millions of Evangelical Christians in America don't feel represented by Jerry Falwell, Pat Robertson, and James Dobson. A lot of Catholics don't feel spoken for by a handful of right-wing bishops telling them there's only one issue on which Catholics can vote. They're saying no. Mainline Protestants feel dismissed by fundamentalists saying they're not people of faith at all. There are rabbis joining us, like Rabbi Steven Jacobs, who is here today.

Wallis paces as he talks, holding the microphone like a pop singer, speaking in a rhythm and tone that is natural, without histrionics (no shouting, no arm-waving) yet dramatic in its sense of urgency, creating a personal rapport that assumes a bond with the audience, a mutual concern. "The right is so happy with the way religion is being interpreted, they act like they own the territory," he says, then pauses, and adds, as if in disbelief at such an outrage, *"that they even own God,"* and goes on:

> They make it simple. Did you know there are only two moral values issues in American politics—abortion and gay marriage? That's it, folks. I am an evangelical Christian and when I find three thousand verses in the Bible about poor people, I insist fighting poverty is a moral value, too. Protecting the environment— otherwise known as God's creation—is a moral value too. And we must insist that the ethics of war—whether you go to war, when you go to war, and when do you tell the truth about going to war—is a religious matter too.
>
> Where would we be if the Reverend Dr. King had kept his faith to himself? I believe in the separation of church and state— but that does not mean the segregation of moral values from public life or the vanishing of all religious language from the public square. We can do this democratically—open, tolerant, welcoming—we don't have to let the right control the territory, nor give it up the way that we've done. We can and must take it back!

Those in the crowd who weren't already standing rise to cheer Wallis's windup; people even put down their lunch boxes to join the ovation. They may not have got a free lunch, but they got a good, free hint of the message and style of two of the leaders who are creating a meaningful response and opposition to the reign of the Religious-Political Right.

† † †

Until the wake-up shock of Bush II's second job renewal and all that it means to my country, I was one of the great slumber party of mainline American Protestant "liberals" (as we were then still known) whose response to the outrages of those who stole our identity as Christians was the cheap and comfortable scorn and smugger-than-thou ridicule of the disengaged. My own religious-political alarm had begun to ring during the summer before the 2004 election, when I reviewed Warren Goldstein's biography *William Sloane Coffin: A Holy Impatience* for *The Nation* magazine. The book brought back to me in stirring detail the work of leaders like Rev. Coffin, Rev. Martin Luther King Jr., Father Daniel Berrigan, and their Jewish allies like the Rabbi Abraham Heschel in battling racism, unjust war, nuclear proliferation, poverty, and threats to civil liberties. I wrote that "Their inspiring example raises a disturbing question: Where are their counterparts now?"

That is the question I asked every religious leader and layperson I spoke with as I traveled around the country in the past year to try to understand what had brought us to the political-religious crisis of our time and what, if anything, was being done about it. The lament of the mainline liberals could be set to the tune of "Mrs. Robinson": "Where have you gone William Sloane Coffin? / A nation turns its lonely eyes to you—hoo-hoo-hoo." When asked who is the contemporary equivalent of Coffin, the white Protestant firebrand of civil rights and the anti-Vietnam movement, several mainline Christians sighed and said, "Well, I guess—Coffin.'"

Long retired from active ministry and in his eighties, Coffin still writes and speaks out against the war in Iraq and the Religious Right more than most mainline leaders today, though he has suffered a stroke and is largely confined to a Barcalounger by the living-room window of his home in New Hampshire. Lacking an active Reverend Coffin, several people suggest his potential successor might be his actual successor at New York's Riverside Church, the popular African-American preacher James Forbes. Both of the people who named Forbes live in New York, though; he has done little to make himself known in the nation at large.

One afternoon over tea in the lounge of the Four Seasons Hotel in Boston, I ask a bright young pastor of a mainline Protestant church in an affluent suburb who he thinks is the contemporary Christian counterpart to William Sloane Coffin in the sixties; after some minutes of silent musing, he shakes his head, then smiles and says, "Rabbi Lerner." This minister is not the only Christian who named the Jewish rabbi as the person who is doing the most significant work in opposing the Religious Right's theft of the meaning and the message of Christianity for the political power of the neocon Republican con men.

The most consistent answer to my question was Jim Wallis, whose barnstorming book tour for his best-selling *God's Politics* took him to fifty-six cities in twenty weeks and brought him into face-to-face question-and-answer sessions with crowds of one to two thousand people at a time. Michael Lerner's new book *The Left Hand of God*—which turns out to be almost a "companion volume" to *God's Politics*—was on target to bring a similar grassroots response at the beginning of 2006.

In many ways an unlikely tandem, Wallis and Lerner, Lerner and Wallis, a rabbi and an Evangelical, are the people most often cited in my homemade, unofficial "poll" of Christians looking for leadership in opposing the Religious Right not only with words but also with deeds.

In terms of money, power, and influence, this is like saying two guys with slingshots are being sent in to battle the billionaire-supported Armies of the Right. But two guys with slingshots are better than nothing, and already their example is inspiring other nonmillionaire, grassroots-level men and women to make their own slingshots and follow.

At least in public they are perfectly cast for the roles of progressive rabbi and preacher who are actively out to "Take Back the Faith" (in Jim Wallis's phrase) from not only the Falwells and Robertsons but the newer and slicker James Dobson and his Focus on the Family (which might more aptly be called Focus on Bashing Gays, Lesbians, and Pro-Choice Advocates), and Senator Bill Frist, George W.'s congressional spokes-bigot, who goes on national television to presume to represent the view of "people of faith."

Wallis and Lerner are not forming any kind of partnership except in the sense of friendly allies who have similar goals. Both men are known as loners, and they don't even agree about the way to go about reaching their common goal of opposing the power of the Religious Right. While Lerner wants to form a "Spiritual Left," Wallis doesn't want to use the term "left," or even "progressive," and least of all "liberal" in his own work.

Wallis tells the crowd at Sproul Hall that he wants to:

go beyond the old categories. "Red" and "Blue" are not biblical categories. Left and right are not a religious framework. People are hungry for a moral center—not a "political middle" like a "mushy center," a place of moral compromise—but a moral center that gets to the heart of an issue, that ends up critiquing both left and right on moral issues, sometimes on one side, sometimes on the other.

Wallis asks me:

> Why would you want to create the Religious Right's exact counterpart on the opposite side? What religion at its best is going to be ideologically predictable or a loyal partisan? There are a lot of people in this nation who we have to reach who do not consider themselves "left" and probably never would—but they will respond to the appeal to find a moral center.

When I speak with him in New Hampshire, William Sloane Coffin says he thinks using the term "Christian Left" or "Religious Left" is simply pragmatic in today's media world:

> You'd get more media coverage if you called yourself a "Christian Left" or "Religious Left" because it's more sensational. If you formed a "Christian Left," the media would flock to you. The problem is that in reality the left is too diffuse, while the right comes across as united. But the media wouldn't care—the media is religiously illiterate. They need to get quick answers.

At this stage, however, as the first meaningful response to the Religious Right is finally taking form, deciding on terminology—left, middle, center, and red, white, or blue—is not the most crucial issue. There's no use debating what flag you will fly under until you have ammunition, troops, and a battle plan, a strategy.

While Lerner worked toward the follow-up conference of his Network of Spiritual Progressives in Washington, D.C., Wallis was making plans to get his message in the press and on the radio on a regular basis.

Wallis tells me:

> Bill Moyers and others say, "'You've helped put out a progressive religious message—not just a progressive political message—now you've got to institutionalize this." So we're talking about a media platform that would involve some kind of radio—we're in discussions with people in radio about a progressive religious show or regular commentaries. Also, I do a lot of op-ed pieces, and we're going to see if one of the syndicates would like a weekly commentary from me on the whole area of religion, values, and ethics. We'll use the Internet very heavily, with much more streaming, much more using speaking events. That's kind of the "air war." James Dobson [founder of the Religious Right's Focus on the Family] is out there on three thousand stations a day, and you need to have a response—not specifically to him, but to have an alternative voice.

Wallis, Lerner, and other religious progressives are up against a long-entrenched and formidable foe, especially on radio and TV. The Republican activist Paul Weyrich told a group of neocon advisers Bush had brought to the White House that they had no excuse for failing to get their message out. "There are fifteen hundred conservative radio talk show hosts. You have Fox News. You have the Internet, where all the successful sites are conservative. The ability to reach people with our point of view is like nothing we have ever seen before." Even if Wallis gets a toehold in radio and television, he realizes that's only a start. "You can't just be on the air and in the media, so we've been having extensive conversations at *Sojourners* about organizational strategies. We've had lots of other organizations and groups come by who'd like to make alliances and partnerships, so we're talking about a pastor's network, a congregational network."

I ask Wallis if he has any plans for trying to do the kind of grassroots political work the Religious Right has done so successfully in getting people elected to school boards and local offices. "I've met lots of local elected officials," he says:

> who have a progressive faith perspective—state senators and representatives, mayors, school board commissioners—they've urged us to have a gathering for state and local officials. We'd have hundreds for such a conference. I've got former students from Harvard running for office around this agenda, running for city councils already, and some of them are going to be running for state offices. The right does it in an overtly partisan way, almost like a power bloc within the Republican Party. I see us doing more like a civil rights movement kind of thing, rather than what the Christian Coalition did. We want to build a

movement around issues like poverty and hold politicians accountable, more than just joining the political party and trying to gain power within the party.

There's going to be many tables out there for forming opposition to the Religious Right. Michael Lerner's group is probably going to be mostly people of a religiously left orientation, like people who are kind of United Church of Christ and Unitarians, and the Mary Ann Williamson kind of spiritual seekers. That's an important group, but you're probably not going to see many Evangelicals there or moderate Catholics.

Michael will be very supportive and nurturing and inspiring to this kind of Religious Left constituency, and some activists who are trying to integrate spirituality with politics. Some are more comfortable with a progressive Jewish response than a Christian one. Michael serves a real role and provides a safe place for progressives who aren't going to be real religious but want to be spiritual.

† † †

We realize this time it's an all-hands-on-deck situation.
—Dave Robinson, director of Pax Christi, the Roman Catholic progressive
movement for peace and justice

The jacket of Robert Edgar's suit is off, and his shirt is crisp and white, his tie straight, his glasses clear. Before becoming general secretary of the National Council of Churches (NCC), Edgar was a six-term member of the House of Representatives, the first Democrat in more than 120 years to be elected from the heavily Republican Seventh District of Pennsylvania. He also has served as a minister to Methodist congregations and as a college chaplain before coming to New York in 2000 to run the NCC from his office in "the God Box" on Upper Broadway. "We've been Sleeping Beauty," he says, "but the actions of the Bush administration to force us into war in Iraq was the kiss that woke us up." One result of the wake-up, Edgar says, is the Web site started by the NCC, called FaithfulAmerica.org (www.faithfulamerica.org). "Is that in response to the Religious Right?" I ask. Edgar sighs:

Almost everything we do is in response to the Religious Right. They have done an excellent job over the last forty years in silencing moderate to progressive voices. We're trying to be silent no more, we're trying to stand up when they're telling us to sit down, and we're trying to speak out when they tell us to be silent. Here we're using some new energy and techniques to go after those that are trying to take us down the wrong road.

We watched how MoveOn.com and Working Assets and other advocacy groups have formulated, and about a year ago we said, Can't we invent that same kind of technology for the faith communities? In May of last year we had two thousand e-mail addresses and now there are over a hundred twenty-five thousand who we talk to about once every ten days. If we had to put a thirty-seven-cent stamp on each letter, [it] would cost us an enormous amount of money. Last week we sent out an alert on Senator Frist when he tried to water down the filibuster—we made a "civil marriage" with some of the Evangelicals and we sent forty-four thousand letters to House and Senate members by simply using e-advocacy and targeting some of the senate offices. If we had five million faithful people across country who cared about the God of creation and stewardship of the planet, if we had five million who cared about the poor—"the least of these"—as brothers and sisters, if we had five million across the country who cared about the beatitude where Jesus says, "Blessed are the peacemakers for they are the children of God," it would change the nature of the country, by having all those people do common action and speak with one voice.

The Right has been organizing effectively for forty years and we've been organizing effectively for three years and it's going to "take us a few more days" to counter them. For thirty years the mainline churches and denominations have been looking internally, not externally. They're more focused on trying to save themselves from being divided on homosexuality, and the Institute for Religion and Democracy and other conservative organizations have been attacking and attacking. The good news about the bad news of churches running out of money is that they have to think more collaboratively about working together, and we're trying to get them to work more closely together to confront the Religious Right and to recognize they've gotta use some practices to build their own congregations. We have a program called Let Justice Roll, and that organization got two million poor people to vote.

Churches that stand for something grow. Not just conservative churches, but liberal churches that take seriously the gospel are increasing in membership. But many of our pastors haven't figured that out yet.

I ask if some of ministers today are fearful of speaking out because of the current atmosphere of divisiveness and the intimidation of the Bush administration and their Religious Right followers. "Absolutely," Bob Edgar says:

> The question I ask is: How do you instill courage and the ability to risk in pastors today? In the sixties, there were a number of pastors willing to be fired over the war in Vietnam and the issues of segregation and civil rights. I see a negative trend recently that many pastors are waiting to retire or don't want to rock the boat in their congregations—they love to tell Bible stories as opposed to taking their spiritual gifts out of the Scripture and relating them to life and work issues. Ministers are under that kind of threat, balancing their call by God to their vocation to the poor and nonviolence and justice with the practical call of where do they get the money to pay their mortgage—it's a serious challenge.

I ask why more ministers risked their jobs to speak out in the sixties. Edgar replies:

> Not all of them were willing, but there were prophetic leaders out there—the Bill Coffins of this world come to mind. There were a number of pastors who modeled that kind of behavior and weren't afraid to go march with Dr. King, including leaders of the Orthodox Church and others. Over time they came to say, "We can't take it anymore." I think the same thing is happening now, but it is happening with a smaller contingent of people and they are not as gifted in using TV as they need to be. TV has

changed a lot since the sixties—this week I was on NBC, MSNBC, and Fox, and I bet only a fraction of our members know that occurred.

I ask if there's anyone comparable now to William Sloane Coffin in liberal religion. Edgar says:

There's a cluster of people who meet every Thursday by telephone. It just started in the last two years, with Jim Wallis, Marian Wright Edelman of the Children's Defense Fund, David Beckman of Bread for the World, George Regas, who was pastor of the big Episcopal Church in Pasadena, Jim Forbes of Riverside Church. The problem with liberals is we don't follow very well. We brand our organizations instead of our issues; the Religious Right is better at branding their issues. We've changed over the last three years, and said there really are only three issues— poverty, environment, justice. All others are important, but we have to brand those issues until we actually see changes in the trend lines on poverty, on the healing of the earth.

"What about the war in Iraq?" I ask. Edgar replies:

It's first . . . I led a delegation to Baghdad, and we sent delegates to talk with Tony Blair, Schroeder, Putin, Chirac, and the pope. Three thousand five hundred people gathered on Martin Luther King's holiday in 2003 to oppose the war, before any body bags were coming back. It was held at the National Cathedral in Washington, and another event at Grace Cathedral in San Francisco. In Vietnam it took years to get opposition to the war, but here before it started most religious leaders were opposed to war—*except our Conservative colleagues, who were reading the Scriptures through the eyes of Armageddon.*

We fell asleep in the seventies, laughed at the early formation of the Moral Majority—we didn't take them seriously. Now the Methodists have a two-million-dollar campaign to try to get people to come to their churches.

The Episcopals and the UCC also have recruitment campaigns, using TV advertising. Now mainline Protestantism has discovered the Internet, whose most successful Web sites are operated by the churches and organizations of the Religious Right, who have had them up and running for decades. They rule the radio airwaves, and as for television, Jan Love of the Methodist Women's Division says:

> Twenty years ago, the mainline Protestant churches made a decision not to get heavily into television—and that was stupid. We didn't know how stupid at the time. Bob Edgar has got us on the Internet. He has also organized meetings with high-level Christian leaders and progressive movements across the country, trying to see if there's a common strategy that can be articulated across the denominations. Bob Edgar is at the heart of those things. And Bill Moyers has helped pull one of these together.

Bob Edgar's work has stirred the Religious Right to label him "Antichrist," which now must be a term of honor among spiritual progressives.

Baptist minister Bill Moyers began the new academic year at Union Theological Seminary in the fall of 2005 by invoking the ghosts of the great teacher-scholars who made that place the bastion of liberal theology—Dietrich Bonhoeffer, Paul Tillich, Reinhold Niebuhr. Moyers said their heritage was now at risk:

> Listen quietly on such an occasion as this and you can hear that chorus of voices—the legions who have passed this way—calling us back to prophetic witness . . . They are saying "Union, religion has bowed again to power and privilege. Stand for justice—and the faith that liberates God from partisan agendas."

Grassroots groups around the country have not required the ghosts of Tillich and Niebuhr to galvanize them; the words of Bush, Rumsfeld, Frist, Falwell, and Robertson have been frightening enough to raise the opposition of ordinary citizens against the current political/religious regime that has led us to war and near–national bankruptcy while invoking a God who stands for war on foreign countries as well as on the middle and lower classes of our own country.

† † †

A group of citizens led by a health care worker rallied in front of the First Baptist Church of Jacksonville, Florida, in August of 2005 to deliver a "declaration to the leaders of the religious right," saying, "You do not speak for us or for our politics. We say 'No' to the way you are using the name and language of Christianity to advance what we see as extremist political goals." The group was organized four months before as the Christian Alliance for Progress (CAP), and held its rally in front of a church ministered by Pastor Jerry Vines, a local Falwell-Robertson clone who had made headlines in 2002 for calling the Prophet Muhammad "a demon-possessed pedophile."

The group's protest against the Religious Right, locally symbolized by Pastor Vines, immediately brought support for CAP from Professor Omid Safi, a cofounder of the Progressive Muslim Union and professor of philosophy and religion at Colgate University, who said the positions taken by CAP reflected those of the PMU and "I think groups like this should be working hand in hand." CAP founder Patrick Mrotek, a health care management consultant, says the group has recruited community organizers in twenty cities across the country and will also join and support the work of Jim Wallis's Call to Renewal movement.

Rev. George Regas, in his twenty-eight years as rector of All Saints Episcopal Church in Pasadena, California, (whose numbers qualify it as a "megachurch") led his congregation to oppose the Vietnam War, the nuclear arms race, and the Gulf War and to support a whole range of human needs, such as an AIDS service center. After retiring from the ministry, he founded and serves as director of Interfaith Communities United for Justice and Peace.

Rev. Regas tells me:

Some people say the reason mainline churches have lost membership is they were too much involved in peace and justice work—

I think they've declined because they haven't done it enough! They've been too timid in that commitment and that's not attractive to anyone. The mainline is timid today—there was a day when it wasn't. In those days we weren't facing a Religious Right—it wasn't part of the story at all. It's sure a new day now. But we can't compete with the Religious Right if we have no financial resources. At least there's a consciousness now in the mainline churches that we have to change and create our own.

Dave Robinson of Pax Christi says: "I think that this is a very hopeful time for progressive religious groups in our country. The events of the past four years have energized some of our traditional groups and have also given birth to new, exciting efforts within the progressive religious community."

These movements are serious, sincere, and dedicated; the meetings of Christian leaders called by Bob Edgar are hopeful, the rhetoric of Wallis and Lerner is inspiring, and even more positive is the fact that they are taking concrete actions. Then look at all these efforts next to just one example of the way the Religious Right is already arming and organizing for the next battle. In August 2005 a Web site appeared that launched the Ohio Restoration Project, whose purpose is to organize thousands of "Patriot Pastors" to get out Religious Right voters for the 2006 elections. The Columbus minister who heads the project calls these midterm congressional elections a battle between "the forces of righteousness and the hordes of hell."

At that same time, the people they call "the hordes of hell" from the NCC—the representatives of mainstream religion—were still trying to agree on a common strategy. Part of the strategy that remains a conundrum to most progressive religious leaders is how not only to avoid the blows from the Armies of the Right but also to overcome the hostility of people who ought to be their allies on the secular left but treat them with scorn, condescension, or indifference.

A young man in Boston came up to Jim Wallis after one of his bookstore talks and said, "I'm gay, and I want to thank you for making me feel welcome tonight, but you know, its easier to come out being gay in Boston than it is coming out as religious in the Democratic Party."

The African-American attorney Van Jones, founder and executive director of the Ella Baker Center for Human Rights in San Francisco (which challenges human rights abuses in the prison system) wrote on the Internet:

> I literally have had liberals laugh in my face when I told them I was a Christian. After a while, I felt self-conscious about telling other activists that I preferred not to come to protests or meetings on Sunday mornings because I wanted to go to church.
>
> It is still commonplace to hear so-called radicals stereotyping all religious people as stupid dupes—and spitting out the word "Christian" like an insult, a disease. I thought progressives were supposed to be the standard bearers of tolerance and inclusion.

The seasoned politician and Union Seminary adviser Scott Harshbarger says:

> You don't go into a liberal community and talk about your faith and your prayers—they snicker. So in divorcing it you lose track

of it, you forget why we should care about social justice—is it just
so we could be fair? What's the underlying principle of equality?
We didn't talk about the values that underlie policy—why are we
against racism, poverty? A lot of these issues I believe in come
from my religious upbringing.

It is difficult at times to know from some of the secular left
attacks on religious figures that the person being skewered
has anything at all in common with progressive politics.
Though the positions Jim Wallis, founder and leader of the
Call to Renewal antipoverty campaign that has organized
many of the nation's churches and church leaders into support
for this overriding cause, takes in his book *God's Politics* are
much the same as those of *The Nation*—against the war in
Iraq and the economic policies and rhetoric of the Bush
administration—Wallis and his book are trashed in *The
Nation* by their star columnist, Katha Pollit, for not having yet
come out for legal abortion and for his explanation of the rea-
soning conservative Evangelicals use to oppose it. Pollitt, who
is known not only for her brilliant prose but also for her hostility to religion, has every right to attack anyone's position on
abortion or anything else that she disagrees with. But is there
no room for acknowledging a common alliance on almost
every other political issue of the day?

In her column "Jesus to the Rescue?," Pollitt admits she
approached Wallis's book *God's Politics* "with a bit of an edge,
having just seen the new film version of *The Merchant of Venice*,
in which the callous anti-Semitism of the Venetian smart set is
rendered with unusual vividness." What has Jim Wallis got to

do with "the Venetian smart set"? Wallis's most prominent friend and ally from another faith, Rabbi Michael Lerner, has not now and has never been a member of the Venetian—or any other—"smart set." Pollit tells us her distress over *The Merchant of Venice* "led me to further gloomy instances, from the Crusades and the Salem Witch Trials to the Magdalene laundries and the antievolution policies of the Dover, Pennsylvania, School Board."

Unaccountably, she left out the Spanish Inquisition in her guilt-by-association practiced on Jim Wallis, but she made up for that with her opinion that "Wallis's evangelicalism is as much a power play as Pat Robertson's," though their politics are diametrically opposed. Not surprisingly, she left out any mention of the many liberal and radical Christians, such as Martin Luther King Jr. and the ministers of the Southern Christian Leadership Conference, Dorothy Day and the Catholic Worker, Rev. William Sloane Coffin, Father Daniel Berrigan, much less St. Francis, St. Theresa of Avila (an early exemplar of women's rights), and that guy they called Jesus, who upset the establishment of his time by preaching peace, turning the other cheek to your enemies, caring for the poor, honoring the outcasts, and even separation of church and state: "Render unto Caesar what is Caesar's, and unto God what is God's."

Pro-choice advocate Jan Love of the Methodist Women's Division says of Pollitt's put-down of Wallis: "It's a mistake for political progressives to flip this guy off when he's an articulate progressive with a very clear biblical heritage—and a book that's on the *New York Times* bestseller list week after week, promoting most of the causes *The Nation* believes in."

Perhaps Pollitt, and the many others on the secular left who don't like anything to do with religion, might take a page from one of the successful strategies of the Religious Right. It is called "cobelligerency." The late Francis Schaeffer, a hard-core Evangelical theologian and guru to archconservatives, promoted this concept to justify Evangelicals making common cause with Roman Catholics on the political issues they agree about: mainly, their opposition to abortion and sex education.

Perhaps the secular left could become "cobelligerents" with religious groups who have the same stand as they do in opposition to the war in Iraq and the Bush administration's policies on the economy as well as civil and human rights, to name a few issues. As "cobelligerents" on such issues, the secular leftists would still be free to consider that their religious partners in a particular alliance were otherwise brainwashed goofballs.

Why can't it work for the religious and secular left, if it worked for the Evangelicals and Catholics?

† † †

In a National Public Radio (NPR) program on the "Relationship between Evangelical Christians and Roman Catholics," host Jennifer Ludden said:

> ever since Martin Luther nailed his thesis to the door of the Wittenberg church, relations between Catholics and Protestants have featured conflict and frequent confrontation, but in the culture wars of contemporary America, traditional Roman Catholics and evangelical Protestants have suddenly found themselves on the same team.

The constitutional attorney Robert Destro of Catholic University noted on the program that "People said in the sixties and seventies, that, you know, 'You better be careful how hard you push in some of these social issues, because if you wake up that sleeping bear, it's going to be a fairly powerful group.'"

NPR religion correspondent Barbara Bradley Hagerty explained:

> Robert Destro says when it comes to life-and-death issues, the beginning of life and the end, there is virtually no light between conservative Catholics and Protestants. That's been the quiet dynamic for years now, he says. What started out as a cobelligerency of two hostiles playing side by side has become a warm and strategic marriage.

Ironically enough, issues within the Roman Catholic Church are not that warm and cozy, especially since the ascension of Cardinal Joseph Ratzinger to the papacy as Benedict XVI. Known for his "silencings" of debate within the Church in his position as chief inquisitor and head of the Congregation of Doctrine and Faith (known until 1965 as the Office of the Holy Inquisition), one of his first actions as pope was to force the Jesuits to remove Rev. Thomas J. Reese as editor of the Catholic magazine *America*. The liberal Catholic journal *Commonweal* lamented that the reaction to the removal of Father Reese was "widespread and impassioned among the Jesuits and in the Catholic academic world. Certainly the Church's reputation has been badly damaged, especially among those in the secular media who knew and had every reason to respect Reese."

Commonweal further feared that if the point of firing Reese was to "send an unmistakable message" about the new pope's policies, then "the self-defeating demand for docility coming from those now in charge in Rome—and increasingly from members of the American episcopate—is only exceeded by their insensitivity and recklessness." Reese's sin as editor was to include other opinions on issues, even though Church doctrine was made most prominent. He published articles on non-Church views of sensitive issues such as stem cell research, same-sex marriage, and whether Catholics who support abortion rights should be refused communion.

Harvard theologian Harvey Cox wrote a book on *The Silencing of Leonardo Boff*, a leader of the Liberation Theology movement of priest-activists who organized and ministered to the poor in Latin America. In his role as chief inquisitor, Ratzinger silenced that movement. The new pope's "silencing" of Father Reese was among the factors that led Professor Cox to tell me:

> I think the age of Catholic dominance in the world may be fading. It may become a smaller group, tighter, more rigid, not really catholic with a small c. It may become more like a sect. They are hemorrhaging to the Pentecostals in Latin America and Africa. Ratzinger—as Pope Benedict XVI—will play well with the right wing—tighten the screws, circle the wagons. John Paul II was a good man, but what did he leave? A shambles.

† † †

The night that Cardinal Joseph Ratzinger was elected pope, Matthew Fox couldn't sleep. Fox had been silenced and then expelled from the Dominican Order after thirty-four years of service, by Cardinal Ratzinger. Ratzinger then shut down the Institute of Culture and Creation Spirituality Fox had created and led, first at Mundelein College in Chicago and then at Holy Names College in Oakland.

After Matthew Fox was shut down by Ratzinger, he opened up his own University of Creation Spirituality, later named Wisdom University, in Oakland. He is now president emeritus and a teaching professor there, as well as a sought-after speaker in the United States and Europe.

Fox was kept awake by the idea that Ratzinger, famous for his "silencings," would become the first pope who had formerly held the position of chief inquisitor in the Vatican. He remembered that he was always telling people to "turn their rage into creativity," so he tried to think how he could do that with his own outrage at Ratzinger's papal ascendancy. It occurred to him that he was going the next month to give lectures at two universities in Germany—the very month Ratzinger would ascend to the papacy. Fox decided that while he was in Germany he would go to Wittenberg and, following the role model of Martin Luther, he would nail some new "theses" against the Roman Catholic Church on the door of the cathedral. He doubted that he could think of ninety-five charges against the Church, as Luther had, but he came up with ten and was able to go to sleep.

Fox woke up again at three in the morning, thinking of more "theses" he could add—and by dawn he had come up with ninety-five. When he went to give his university lectures in Germany, Fox took a side trip to Wittenberg, called up all the TV stations, and invited them to watch him nail up the ninety-five theses of what he calls "the New Reformation."

Fox is a lean, white-haired man who electrified the crowd at the *Tikkun* conference for Spiritual Progressives in Berkeley. "It's not just the Catholic Church that's in trouble today," Fox told the audience, "The Protestant churches are wimpy! The mainline Protestant churches have lain down and let that 'kooky Christianity' roll right over them and steal Jesus' name and steal Christ's name and carry on an immoral version of religion—a religion of domination instead of justice."

Fox offered a solution to the internal religious wars that are tearing apart denominations in America today. "I think its time for a divorce," he said:

> I really do. Divorces are sometimes necessary, and we don't have to be vicious about it. I think the distinction is there to see—those who want to worship a dominating, punitive father-God, which is of course a put-down of women, gays, nature—and those who want to worship a Wisdom God who is a mother-father God, and who is embedded in nature, and in the creativity of our bodies, of all our art forms, lined up on one side or the other. Instead of trying to keep our little churches together, or our denominations, why not let them go their way? We will regroup with a lot more energy to the real issues of our time, like economic justice, gender

justice, preserving the environment. For me it's a choice between necrophilia and biophilia.

The roomful of "spiritual progressives" stood up and cheered.

† † †

"We Are The Ones We Have Been Waiting For."

There is a split coming in the Evangelical movement, and it's a very significant one. Tony Campolo, one of the most articulate progressive Evangelical leaders, tells me, "I think it's imminent. The challenge is to draw the whole thing together. Jim Wallis has his followers from the Call to Renewal movement, as well as readers of his book and of *Sojourners* magazine. I've been putting together a pretty good following of progressive Evangelicals myself."

Campolo, a professor emeritus of sociology at Eastern University in St. Davids, Pennsylvania, is founder of the Evangelical Association for the Promotion of Education (EAPE), a popular speaker, and author of books including *Which Jesus?, Speaking My Mind,* and *Following Jesus without Embarrassing God.*

Campolo tells me:

> Brian McLaren [another popular Evangelical minister and author] has been gathering support from a new movement called the Emerging Church. There's a need to coalesce and put these movements together along with others who want an alternative.

Thirty-five or thirty percent of the Evangelical community falls into this category, and that's still *millions* of Christians. We think we can make it happen. Jim Wallis and Brian McLaren and I get together regularly, and we just decided that every Tuesday morning at eight o'clock in the morning we're going to have a phone conference, see where we're at, see what's happening, how to begin to move and coalesce, and become a dynamic force. September 13 [2005] was our first conference call.

Campolo predicts that by the spring of 2006:

We ought to be hopping and rolling. This will involve both churches and individuals. If you looked at the Christian Coalition, it involved all these things. We will do the same—there will be individuals who will want to be a part of this, and there will be churches who will want to align with us. The time has come. We've been playing softball up to this point, but the time has come to play hardball. We would call ourselves Evangelicals insofar as we can use the term—we hate to give the term away. At the same time, we recognize the term is losing its meaning. The popular mind identifies Evangelicals with the Religious Right. We may not be able to use the term any more. We may have to go and start using Brian McLaren's term, "the Emergent Church," simply because it differentiates us.

I ask if the Emergent Church is Evangelical. "Yes," Campolo says:

and when we say "Evangelical," I need to define what we mean by that. We mean these things—first of all, we believe in the Apostles Creed, we think that's a good doctrinal statement. Secondly, we talk about and try to invite people into a personal relationship with Jesus. We really believe that's what's been missing in mainline denominations—that personal involvement with Christ. And the third thing is that we have a very high view of Scripture, we believe it's the right guide for faith and practice. Those three things are what characterize where we're coming from and what we've got to say.

I ask if this new group will be part of the National Association of Evangelicals (NAE). Campolo replies:

I think we'd like to be in a close association with them. The problem with the NAE is that they say all the great things we are for—they are for protecting the environment, they are for ending poverty—they are for these great causes. The problem is that the minute you get down to concrete politics, they want to remain silent. Here's what I mean: do you want to take a stand against Bush when he deregulates the automotive industry and the factories of this country so they can emit more poisons into the atmosphere? The deregulation that is going on under the Bush administration has been frightening. Are we willing to speak out against Bush on this issue? Well, at this point the NAE will get very nervous. So what does it mean to say: "We are out to protect the environment but we don't want to say anything negative about the Bush administration and its policies on this matter?"

Leaders of the NAE felt they were being embarrassed by

Jerry Falwell and Pat Robertson, and they felt they needed to do something to say: "That's not who we are." At the same time, they recognize that a significant proportion of their constituency *identifies* with the likes of Robertson and Falwell. So they have to walk this thin line: "How do we escape being tarred with the same image Robertson and Falwell have without losing a significant support base that we need to keep our organization alive and functioning?"

The Religious Right has defined environmentalism as a kind of New Age movement and they're very nervous about it. They're nervous about *me*—and they're nervous about me for a good reason. That is that certain Evangelicals have become concerned that I'm too soft on the gay issue. So they want to make sure they don't get too close to me lest they end up with that designation. I'm conservative on the issue, it's just that I believe there's a homophobia running through Evangelicalism that needs to be challenged. They're nervous about that. They want me to be a distant cousin.

I've served in the past on committees with the NAE but I only have so much energy to expend. So one has to ask oneself— and I think Jim [Wallis] feels this same way—does it make much sense to try to move the National Association of Evangelicals into having a better image? Or does it make more sense to spend our energies trying to create a movement to countervail that whole Religious Right mentality? If we had the time, I'm sure I would go to NAE meetings, and so would Jim Wallis, and we would make our voices heard there—but we don't have the time to do it all.

I'll tell you who is very interested in connecting with Call to

Renewal and Jim Wallis—this will surprise you—it's Bill Hybel
at Willow Creek.

Hybel is the founder and pastor of the Willow Creek Community Church, in South Barrington, Illinois, outside Chicago,
which grew from a rented movie theater in 1975 to a
megachurch with more than a hundred acres of land and build-
ings and more than a hundred kinds of "ministries" for parishioners. "Bill Hybel reached out to Jim," Campolo says. "As you
can see, there's a shaking of the foundations out there. Bill
Hybel doesn't want to be identified with Jerry Falwell and Pat
Robertson and James Dobson. He was on Jim Dobson's board
and has resigned."

Another key leader joining this new movement is Wesley
Granberg-Michaelson, head of the Reformed Church in
America, a denomination that is theologically Evangelical in
some of its churches and not in others. Granberg-Michaelson tells
me that this new movement with Wallis, Campolo, and McLaren,
using Wallis's Call to Renewal and *Sojourners* followers as a base:

> will be broader than just Evangelicals—there will be a great
> many Evangelicals and it will incorporate many other Christians
> committed to what we feel are solid, biblically grounded ways on
> the kind of social issues that deal with poverty, peace, and justice—
> and at the same time recognize the real important role of family,
> the role of personal morality, without saying the only people who
> have the integrity to talk about those issues are the far right,
> which doesn't make sense.

Granberg-Michaelson believes that the people who will be led as Christians in the causes of social justice, peace, and poverty will play a key role in supporting those issues—just as the "soldiers" of the Armies of the Right have served in the trenches for what Mathew Fox calls "the kooky Christianity" of the Falwells and Robertsons and their ilk. "People who are convinced that they're following a biblical call, following a mandate of their faith and discipleship on questions before society have the most powerful motivation of all," Granberg-Michaelson says:

> It's a motivation that's more than just political, that's why it's so important to clarify the biblical and discipleship nature of how we engage in this task. We don't engage in efforts addressing questions of society and the world out of a kind of political motivation —we do it because we're following Jesus. I think a lot of Protestant liberals have grown uncomfortable with that kind of language—but at the end of it all, it's following Jesus in the world, and we've given our lives to this, given our lives to God's purposes in the world. That's the most powerful motivation of all, and I think that's what has to be recovered.

Granberg-Michaelson, who served on the staff of Senator Mark Hatfield of Oregon and worked with Jim Wallis as managing editor of *Sojourners* from 1976 to 1978, is also the chair of the steering committee of a new organization called Christian Churches Together in the USA (CCT), the most inclusive group of a variety of Christian faiths to be formed in the United States, from Pentecostals to Roman Catholics, Orthodox churches, and mainline denominations that belong to the National Council of Churches, whose general secretary Robert Edgar endorses the new CCT. The leaders of the Religious Right aren't interested.

Granberg-Michaelson tells me:

> Our intention was not to respond to the one monolithic voice of the Church on the far right. That wasn't why CCT was formed—however, in the Evangelical-Pentecostal community there's a growing number who really differentiate themselves from the far right and are really interested in seeking a wider unity of purpose.
>
> Falwell, Robertson, and the Southern Baptists are not interested in being part of Christian Churches Together. We haven't heard from Robertson and Falwell, nor would we expect that this would be the kind of opportunity they'd be looking for.
>
> The media has just talked about the Religious Right and People for the American Way sometimes—as if there were no other kinds of Christians. It used to be the media didn't know what an Evangelical was, and then it got so fascinated they thought all Evangelicals were like Pat Robertson and Jerry Falwell. The media still has a heavy learning curve on this.

† † †

Jim Wallis says:

> There are beginning to be alliances with Catholics who don't feel represented by a handful of right-wing issues—tell them

there is only one issue on which Catholics can vote and say
"No." Latinos and blacks and lot of rabbis are coming out.
There are a lot of young Muslims who want peace—this is an
internal issue within their faith—all the great religions have a
battle within them between fundamentalism and prophetic
faith, in Islam and Judaism and Christianity. A whole lot of
young people say, "I'm not religious but I'm spiritual, and I
want to be in this conversation too." A lot of people say, "I'm
secular, agnostic, I'm even atheist but I want to be a part of a
moral discourse on politics."

Every single progressive movement in our history—abolition
of slavery, women's suffrage, child labor laws, civil rights—were
all driven and fueled in large part by religion, faith, spirituality.
We have a proud progressive spiritual history. It's ours—we did
it before—and we can do it again. The time for the Religious
Right is passing now, and our time has finally come.

Wallis quotes a young black woman activist in D.C. who
didn't want to wait for others to carry out Jesus' teachings to
help the poor and the outcasts; she told her fellow workers for
peace and justice and the fight against poverty that "We are the
ones we have been waiting for."

Whether the secular left or the Democrats like it or not, 90
percent of the country is religious, and now that religion has
entered the political dialogue—has become the *focus* of political
dialogue—they had better deal with it, in more than phrases
and lip service. Some of them are doing it. Both Hillary Clinton
and John Edwards are in continuous dialogue with the principle Evangelical progressives, and the plans of these leaders for

religious realignment is going to have an effect on the political map of this country.

Perhaps an even wider majority could be formed among not only those who believe in Jesus but also those who don't, but who believe in the causes he preached of caring for the poor and the outcasts of society. Most of the Religious Right has cast aside those teachings, instead politically empowering the wealthy and attacking society's current outcasts of gays, lesbians, and sexual minorities.

Most of the world's Christians believe that one of the principal gifts of their faith is the message Jesus gave to the multitudes on the mountain—a message that many on the Religious Right have declared is no longer a part of their belief:

> Blessed are the poor in spirit: for theirs is the kingdom of heaven.
> Blessed are they that mourn: for they shall be comforted.
> Blessed are the meek, for they shall inherit the earth.
> Blessed are they which do hunger and thirst after righteousness:
>   for they shall be filled.
> Blessed are the merciful for they shall obtain mercy.
> Blessed are the pure in heart: for they shall see God.
> Blessed are the peacemakers: for they shall be called the children
>   of God.

Acknowledgments

Thanks to Amanda Hoffman, Melanie Neal, Molly McGreevy, Jennifer Hearn, Andy Cohen, Wayne Cowan, Leon Howell, Donna Schaper, Warren Goldstein, Carl Scovel, Norm Eddy, Bill and Chris Chapman, Ted Steeg, Mimi Mindel, Gene and Fay Hale, Morton Mintz, and other friends and generous people who helped along the way, including all who took the time to be interviewed, and also to my wonderful goddaughter, Karina Perez Corrales, whose presence in my life is a gift.

INDEX

See also civic responsibility; civil rights
  movement; Vietnam War protests;
  women's liberation movement
social issues
  ethics of war, 163
  Evangelical focus, 38, 55–56, 98, 100,
    102, 104
  letting go of denominations in favor of
    dealing with, 186–187
  marriage, male dominance and violence
    in, 58–59
  See also abortion; civil rights; homosexu-
    ality; poverty
Sojourners (magazine), 2, 21, 57
Solomon, Deborah, 42
spiritual progressives
  conference, 104–106, 108, 112, 124,
    186–187
  Network of Spiritual Progressives, 168
  See also progressive faith perspectives
spiritual warfare, U.S. military and, 25–26
Spong, John Shelby, 141
St. John's Episcopal Church (Washington,
  D.C.), 14–15
Stanley, Charles, 22
stewardship of creation, 40–41
Stewart, Jon, 159
Still Speaking Initiative (UCC campaign), 10
Sugg, John F., 22

T
television, mainline churches's failure to uti-
  lize, 175
Theonomy movement, 26–27
Thomas, Clarence, Justice, 82
Tikkun Community, 160
Tikkun (magazine)
  conference sponsored by, 104–106, 108,
    112, 124, 186–187
  Lerner and, 160
tolerance, unacceptability of, 138–140
Tooley, Mark, 117
Towne, Anthony, 71–72

U
UCC (United Church of Christ), 7, 120–122
Union Theological Seminary, 11, 67–68, 176
Unitarian-Universalist Association (UUA),
  122–124

United Church of Christ (UCC), 7, 120–122
United Methodism at Risk (Howell), 91
United Methodist Church
  on abortion, 103
  on homosexuality, 114–115
  investigation of IRD, 91–92
  IRD's takeover mission, 92–93, 96–97,
    98–100
  Ku Klux Klan attacks on, 67–68
  Reconciling Ministries Network, 115,
    116–117
  See also Johnson, Kathryn
unsaved versus saved, 17–18, 36
U.S. armed forces, Boykin's spiritual war-
  fare approach, 25–26
UUA (Unitarian-Universalist Association),
  122–124

V
Vahanian, Gabriel, 72
van Buren, Paul, 71, 72
Venezuela, Robertson's desire to assassinate
  president of, 34, 59–60
Vietnam War protests
  as "antipathy to what U.S. represented," 45
  Christian activism, mixed repercussions
    from, 70
  mainline church support as contributing
    to downfall, 78–79
  ministers' willingness to be fired for, 173
  Regas participation in, 177
  slow development of, 174–175
  Sunday School plastered for food relief
    to Vietnam, 90–91
Vines, Jerry, 177

W
Wakefield, Dan, 164
Wald, Kenneth, 14
Wallis, Jim
  on alliances among spiritual believers,
    193–194
  on battle between fundamentalism and
    prophetic faith, 102, 193–194
  as caller of Evangelicals long before they
    would listen, 56–57
  Call to Renewal program, 160–161
  on common ground for abortion issue,
    104–106